an illustrated history of Aircraft

GALAHAD
gb
★ ★
BOOKS

Published in the United States of America
in 1981 by A & W Publishers, Inc.
95 Madison Avenue
New York, New York 10016
By arrangement with Quarto Publishing
Limited

ISBN 0 88365 482 2

This book was designed and produced by
Quarto Publishing Limited, 32 Kingly Court,
London W1

Phototypeset in England by Filmtype Services
Limited, Scarborough
Colour separation by Sakai Lithocolour
Company Limited, Hong Kong
Printed by Leefung-Asco Printers Limited,
Hong Kong

CONTENTS

THE
HISTORY
OF
FLIGHT

Dassault Mirage F1 single-seat multi-mission fighters and attack aircraft

MAN BECOMES AIRBORNE

IT IS UNLIKELY we shall ever know the name of the person to first comment that if God had intended men to fly he would have given them wings. It could, quite easily, have been the Chinese spectator of an unsuccessful launch of a man-lifting kite, perhaps one or more centuries before the birth of Christ. That is a realistic date for the first men to become airborne, and the desire to fly like the birds could well stretch back to prehistoric man, conscious of the ease with which winged creatures could elude land-bound predators.

Myth and fantasy fill the years that come between the wishes of those prehistoric ancestors and the first of the thinking men to consider seriously, but unsuccessfully, the mechanics of flight. Leonardo da Vinci (1452–1519), Italian artist-inventor, produced many designs for ornithopter (flapping-wing) aircraft but prudently made no practical experiments. A hundred and fifty years after his death, in 1670, a Jesuit priest, Francesco de Lana-Terzi, had heard of the invention of the vacuum pump. This seemed to him to offer a possibility of flight, based upon the assumption that a thin metallic globe from which the air had been evacuated could be lighter than air and thus would float in the air. He failed to see the simple fact, about which most present-day school children could have advised him, that if his metallic spheres had been light enough to lift they would have been crushed by atmospheric pressure at the moment of evacuation.

The first lighter-than-air craft

Since schooldays most of us have believed that the brothers Etienne and Joseph Montgolfier were the first to launch a hot-air balloon. Recent research has shown that another priest, the Brazilian Bartolomeu de Gusmão, demonstrated a practical model of a hot-air balloon at the court of King John V of Portugal, in 1709. On 8 August that year, before a distinguished gathering of reliable witnesses, de Gusmão showed the amazed audience that his small paper balloon, with burning material suspended below the open neck of the envelope, could rise in free flight within the confines of the Ambassador's drawing-room. Its brief journey was brought to an end when two servants, fearing it might set the curtains alight, dashed it to the ground. A lighter-than-air craft had thus been demonstrated 74 years before the first flight of a Montgolfier hot-air balloon took place.

This in no way detracts from the achievements of the Montgolfiers. Their first hot-air balloon was launched, prob-

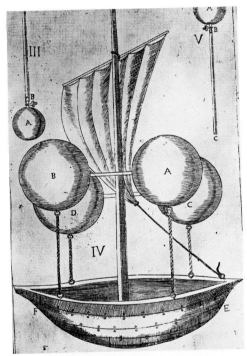

Bladud, (above), fabled ninth king of Britain, was an early 'jumper', who fixed artificial wings to his arms. De Lana Terzi's flying-machine (centre), was also a non-starter. The work of men like Leonardo da Vinci (right) gave a starting point to later thinkers. The first free flight in a *Montgolfière* (left) was undertaken by de Rozier and the Marquis d'Arlandes. The engraving (far right) records de Rozier's fatal cross-Channel attempt in a composite hot-air/hydrogen balloon. Both de Rozier and his companion Jules Romain were killed.

ably at Annonay, France, on 25 April 1783. Some 12 m (39 ft) in diameter, it climbed to a height of about 305 m (1,000 ft) before the hot air in the envelope cooled and it began its descent. The Montgolfier brothers are said to have been unaware that hot air alone was the lifting agent for their balloons, believing that a specially light gas was generated by the mixture of wool and straw which they burned below the open neck of the envelope.

A second demonstration, at Annonay, was given on 4 June 1783, but just prior to a third, command performance at the Court of Versailles on 19 September of that same year, when a sheep, a duck and a cock became the first living creatures to be artificially airborne, Professor J. A. C. Charles had demonstrated successfully a small hydrogen-filled balloon at Paris, on 27 August 1783.

Events were then to move quickly. On 15 October 1783 Francois Pilâtre de Rozier became the first man in the world to be carried aloft, sole passenger of a Montgolfier balloon tethered to the ground by a 26 m (84 ft) rope. Just over a month later, on 21 November 1783, de Rozier accompanied by the Marquis d'Arlandes, made the first free flight in a balloon, remaining airborne for 25 minutes, during which time they travelled about 8·5 km (5·5 miles) from their launch point. Free flight in a lighter-than-air craft had at last been realised. And although this was a beginning, it was also virtually the end of the Montgolfier balloon, superseded by the infinitely superior and practical hydrogen-filled balloon developed by J. A. C. Charles, in which he and one of the Robert brothers who had assisted in its construction made a free flight from the gardens of the Tuileries, Paris, on 1 December 1783. Their flight was one of 43 km (27 miles), their ascent witnessed by a crowd estimated at some 400,000, their balloon so well designed that it is essentially similar to the gas-filled balloon used to this day.

Making the balloon navigable

The expansion of ballooning as a sport was very rapid: at last man was free of the Earth which had been his habitat for so many centuries. There was no telling what achievements might now be possible. And within days of de Rozier's first flight in a

Montgolfière had come an appreciation of the potential which such a vehicle held for military pursuits, especially for reconnaissance. But there had to be some method of steering, for the balloon was possessed by the least zephyr. Grandiose ideas involving oars, sails and propellers were of no avail; it had to be understood that if an airborne vehicle was to be steerable it must be capable of independent movement, instead of being carried by the wind, so that movable aerofoil surfaces could impose a chosen direction of travel. From this realisation stemmed the initial airship designs, the envelope becoming elongated instead of spherical, with the provision of a power plant to provide forward motion independently of the breeze. This latter word is chosen advisedly: there was then no question of trying to fly in anything that might be classed as a wind.

The major problem, and the one which was to frustrate the pioneers of heavier-than-air craft, was the non-availability of a suitable lightweight and compact power plant. Thus, Frenchman Henri Giffard, who recorded the first flight of a manned, powered dirigible (Latin: 'able to be directed') on 24 September 1852, utilised a 2·2 kW (3 hp) steam-engine, driving a 3·35 m (11 ft) diameter propeller. The use of the word 'dirigible' in that record is rather open to question, for anything more than the merest suggestion of a breeze would have made it unsteerable. To Charles Renard and Arthur Krebs, officers of the French Corps of Engineers, goes the distinction of flying *La France*, the world's first fully controllable and powered dirigible. In this craft, on 9 August 1884, Renard and Krebs flew a circular course of about 8 km (5 miles), taking off from and returning to Chalais-Meudon, France. Powered by a 6·7 kW (9 hp) Gramme electric motor, driving a 7·01 m (23 ft) diameter propeller, *La France* achieved a maximum speed of 23·5 km/h (14·5 mph) during its 23 minute flight. Increased power had provided the speed necessary to make the vehicle controllable: but this seemingly small improvement had taken 101 years from the first flight of the Montgolfier balloon.

The first heavier-than-air craft

The beginning of heavier-than-air flight is the story of many men working towards a common goal. As in most combined and

international projects, there are men who stand out because of their advanced thoughts or brilliant innovations.

First must come the man now regarded as the 'Father of Aerial Navigation', the English Baronet Sir George Cayley (1773–1857). Back in 1804 he built what is generally regarded as the first successful model glider. This consisted of little more than a broomstick to which was mounted a kite-shape monoplane wing; at the aft end of the 'fuselage' were vertical and horizontal tail surfaces to provide control. With this device he was able to confirm that the principles of heavier-than-air flight were entirely feasible, and it was able to demonstrate stable flight over quite long distances.

From this first model he evolved gliders capable of carrying a small schoolboy in flight (1849), and his reluctant coachman during 1853. Both were passengers only, with no means of controlling their aircraft in flight. But in addition to his practical work, Cayley suggested the use of an internal combustion engine for powered flight, demonstrated how a curved aerofoil surface provides lift, and pointed out that biplane or triplane wings would provide maximum lift from a lightweight, robust structure. Cayley's 'Father' title was well-earned.

Cayley died in 1857, and in that same year a French naval officer, Félix du Temple, constructed and flew the world's first powered model aeroplane. This record was achieved with a clockwork motor, and subsequently du Temple's little monoplane was powered with a steam-engine. Seventeen years later this same inventor was flight testing a full-size man-carrying aeroplane, which was powered by either a hot-air engine or a steam-engine. Piloted by an unknown sailor, at Brest, this aircraft was the first in the world to achieve a short hop into the air, following launch down an inclined ramp.

Although men were beginning to learn how to construct a fixed-wing aircraft that could fly, their problem was now the same as that of the balloonist who wanted to steer his vessel: both needed a suitable power plant. A practical working layout for a suitable power plant was to be demonstrated by the German engineer Nicholas Otto, in 1876. The four-stroke cycle of operations for an internal combustion engine, which Otto evolved at that

THE EARLIEST DAYS

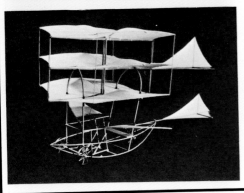

Cayley's model glider (*top, left*), with its adjustable aerofoil surfaces, enabled him to experiment with the problems of gliding flight, leading to the 'boy lifter' of 1849 (*left*). Clément Ader's *Éole* steam-powered

monoplane (*top*) was the first aircraft to lift itself from the ground, but failed to fly. Félix du Temple's monoplane (model *above*) made a short hop after launch down a ramp, powered by a hot-air or steam engine.

time, is still the basic principle upon which most piston-engines work, especially for motor cars and aircraft. But Otto's invention was in the future. The more practical among the pioneer aviators accepted the reality of the situation, and spent the period most profitably in improving airframe design, learning the best means of lightweight construction, and trying to discover practical means of controlling the aircraft when it became airborne.

The beginning of free flight

The most important of this group of pioneers was the German Otto Lilienthal (1848–1896), whose beautifully built lightweight gliders enabled him to make many thousands of flights. These were not just pleasure flights: Lilienthal was a prac-

tical researcher, building, modifying, improving, and at all times recording meticulously the results of his experiments for the benefit of other researchers.

Lilienthal's gliders were of the configuration which we would now call hang-gliders, designed so that the mass of his body was disposed about the aircraft's centre of gravity when the machine was in a stable flying position. By body movements he could influence a degree of control on the craft's flight but, unfortunately, this did not allow rapid response to changing flight conditions. Despite his experience, Lilienthal was gravely injured in a flying accident on 9 August 1896, brought about by a control problem which could not be resolved quickly enough, and he died on the following day.

Lilienthal had been a source of inspiration to many, but influenced especially the work of the British pioneer builder/pilot Percy Pilcher (1866–1899), who flew his first glider in 1895. Pilcher travelled to Germany to meet and talk with Otto Lilienthal, from whom he obtained a great deal of practical advice. But Pilcher, too, was to die on 30 September 1899, when his *Hawk* glider crashed to the ground at Market Harborough.

There was a third important glider pioneer—a builder not a flyer—who collected information from every possible source, publishing this *pot-pourri* under the title *Progress in Flying Machines*. American railway engineer, Octave Chanute (1832–1910), the compiler of this book, was to develop the Lilienthal-

Hiram Maxim's giant steam-powered craft (*below*), spanning 31·7 m (104 ft) developed so much lift that it broke away from its safety rails. At the same time Germany's Otto Lilienthal (*right*) was flying well-built hang-gliders. Despite an advanced engine, Langley's *Aerodrome* (*bottom left*) failed to fly, both attempts at flight ending in the river.

type craft into a classic glider. More importantly for powered flight, his book, his advice and his friendship, were to inspire the brothers Orville and Wilbur Wright.

There are many links in the chain of progress towards the realisation of powered flight, some big and many small. All contribute to the end result, and it is unfortunate that space will not allow us to relate them all. One of the final links was undoubtedly Germany's Gottlieb Daimler, who in 1885 developed the world's first single-cylinder internal combustion engine. This utilised the four-stroke principle of operation devised by his fellow countryman, Nicholas Otto, and used petrol as its fuel. As it was developed to provide a power-to-weight ratio far superior to any other form of engine then available for aircraft propulsion, the would-be aviators realised that the necessary power-plant had arrived.

But this was to be of no avail to American Samuel Pierpont Langley, the man who so nearly made the Wright brothers just aviation pioneers. Langley was a scientist, Secretary of the Smithsonian Institution, and his collaboration with Charles Manley to build and fly his *Aerodrome* aircraft resulted in the creation by

Manley and his associate Stephen Balzer of a remarkably advanced five-cylinder radial petrol-engine. Despite this advantage, Langley's aircraft failed to become airborne on two occasions. Both times — 7 October and 8 December 1903 — the aircraft crashed into the Potomac River. Most observers believed the *Aerodrome* fouled its launching device on both dates, but it has been suggested that the aircraft's structure disintegrated. Either way, the stage was clear for the Wright brothers.

The historic picture (*below*) is of the first flight of the Wright *Flyer* on 17 December 1903. Orville Wright, who was at the controls, later wrote: *The course of the flight up and down was exceedingly erratic. The control of the front rudder* (elevator) *was difficult. As a result, the machine would rise suddenly to about ten feet, and then as suddenly dart for the ground. A sudden dart when a little over*

Powered flight becomes reality

The achievement of that cold Thursday, 17 December 1903, has been told so many times that much of the excitement has gone. Except, perhaps, for those who have learned to fly: who understand that moment of magic when the aircraft loses contact with the ground and becomes a living creature, free in three-dimensional space: so very nearly a bird in flight.

The brothers Orville and Wilbur deserved their success, because of their de-

120 feet from the point at which it rose into the air ended the flight. **Three others followed, the last and best of that day covering 260 m (852 ft), but ended with the elevator being damaged when the *Flyer* landed. When it was overturned by a gust of wind more damage followed. The ironical feature of these flights was that the world failed to learn that a man had been airborne and in control of a powered**

termination to overcome the very real difficulties that beset them. If they hadn't got it they made it; if it didn't work, they found out why and changed their design.

And when the *Flyer* was dismantled on that historic day it was an end to the first phase of powered flight. The world's first powered, sustained and controlled flight had been accomplished. It was also a beginning: the expansion of aviation to facilitate world travel and inaugurate a hoped-for era of peace.

heavier-than-air craft. It was not until three years later, in November 1906, that the little Brazilian Alberto Santos-Dumont electrified aviation progress in Europe by recording a first flight in his No. 14-*bis* of nearly 61 m (200 ft). Both aircraft were really dead-end designs, but their achievement and influence inspired new ideas and efforts. In the short-term, more powerful engines were the key to success.

PIONEERS OF POWERED FLIGHT

IT IS IRONICAL that the 'beginning' with which we closed the last chapter was then, so far as the world is concerned, no beginning at all. In fact, it was not until almost three years later, on 23 October 1906, when the Brazilian Alberto Santos-Dumont achieved a flight of nearly 60 m (200 ft), in Paris, that the world realised the first flight of a powered heavier-than-air craft had been accomplished. This was because the flight was observed by thousands, photographed and recorded in the world's newspapers. Almost three weeks later, on 12 November, he covered 220 m (722 ft) in the same aircraft, his so-called '14-*bis*'.

Santos-Dumont's aircraft was a strange-looking machine, with box-kite-like wings. It seemed even more odd when it was realised that it flew with the tail way out in front and the wings at the back. This configuration has earned the name 'canard', because such craft have some resemblance to a duck in flight. The box-kite wings stemmed from the original research of Lawrence Hargrave in Australia. Hargrave had perfected the design of the box-kite in 1893, and the lightweight and robust construction of this device, together with its good lifting characteristics, encouraged a number of European designers to adopt this form of structure for their early attempts to build the ideal aircraft.

By 1907, the Wright design was beginning to have an influence upon European constructors, leading to a combination of Wright features with the Hargrave box-kite. In reality, it was a dead-end design, with only a short road for its followers to travel. It is worth explaining at this point that the power plant of the above aircraft was mounted so that the propeller was not only behind the engine, but also aft of the main wing structure. The arrangement was called, somewhat inaccurately, a pusher propeller.

New designs emerging in Europe were quite different, comprising monoplane and biplane aircraft with the engine mounted at the forward end of the fuselage and the propeller at the front of the engine. This was known as a tractor configuration, the propeller pulling the entire machine through the air. A little thought will bring the realisation that the propeller in a pusher configuration is doing exactly the same thing, but it has proved convenient—even to this day—to call the forward-mounted propeller a tractor, and the aft-mounted version a pusher.

By the beginning of 1908 there was some progress in Europe, but control of

Noting the marginal capability of such aircraft as Santos-Dumont's 14-*bis*, other pioneers examined new ideas to achieve the aim of 'flight like the birds'. Paul Cornu's twin-rotor helicopter (*top left*) recorded the first rotary-wing flight on 13 November 1907; the Ecquevilly multi-plane (*left*) was one of the proposals to gain more lift from short span; Karl Jatho's aircraft (*top right*) was nearly the first to fly in Germany; Trajan Vuia's machine (*above*) could only hop.

By 1908, when Wilbur Wright demonstrated the *Flyer A* (*below*) in France, the two brothers had refined its design almost to the ultimate. In Europe the pioneers were still trying to evolve a really practical aeroplane. Aircraft such as the Koechlin Boxkite (*right*) and Blériot/Voisin with cellular wings (*below right*) owed much to the work of the Australian Lawrence Hargrave.

the aircraft in flight had not graduated beyond the elementary stage. Men were airborne in powered aircraft, but their flight was far from emulating that of a bird: they were more akin to tightrope walkers, certainly in the air, but very limited in their flight pattern. To illustrate the point, the first flight to exceed one minute's duration had been recorded by Henry Farman, flying his Voisin-Farman I biplane on 10 November 1907. On 13 January 1908 the same combination of aircraft and pilot recorded completion of the first 1 km (1·6 miles) circle flown in Europe, in a time of 1 min 28 sec. At the then current stage of aviation development on the East side of the Atlantic, this was no mean achievement, and won for Henry Farman the 50,000 francs Deutsch/Archdeacon Grand Prix d'Aviation. But changes were imminent.

The moment of truth
In the summer of 1908 Wilbur Wright visited France, bringing with him a Wright *Flyer A*, with which to give a series of demonstration flights. He based himself initially at Hunaudières, near Le Mans, and very soon had uncrated and assembled his aircraft.

On 8 August, in the cool, windless, near-twilight of that summer evening, he prepared to take off before a highly critical audience of European—mostly French—pilots. Collectively they considered themselves the hub of aviation development and achievement. After all, there was really no certainty that the Wrights had flown prior to the great

achievement of Santos-Dumont. And, with a nudge of the elbow: "You know how these Yankees exaggerate."

There was a sudden roar from the engine, focusing attention, but by then Wilbur and the *Flyer* were airborne. But look, here indeed is the legendary birdman, climbing, turning, banking with unbelievable perfection and grace. Man and machine are one, weaving dream patterns in a sunset sky. The audience is silent, breathless, eyes almost blinded by emotion. Too soon it is ended as, with engine throttled back, Wilbur sets the *Flyer* calmly and gracefully on the ground. The spectators are still silent, still breathless. Then suddenly the cheers ring out; of amazement, of appreciation, of congratulation. Wilbur has demonstrated, convincingly, the considerable lead which the Wrights then held in aviation capability and their

mastery of control. From that moment forward European aviation was spurred to progress in leaps and bounds.

New achievements: new power
The European pilots were soon to discover that Wilbur was indeed one of the brotherhood, prepared to talk about design and improvements, and his demonstrations and influence had a profound effect on the rapid development of European aviation. By the end of 1908, flying from Auvours, France, Wilbur had made more than 100 flights totalling in excess of 25 flying hours. His last flight of the year, on 31 December, occupied 2 hrs 20 min 23 sec, during which he covered a distance of 124 km (77 miles) to set a new world record and win the Michelin prize.

And while Wilbur was busy in Europe, Orville Wright was demonstrating at Fort

Three aircraft showing evolutionary changes in basic design. The Voisin (*top*) is typical of the structure evolved from the box-kite. Farman's biplane (*above*) shows a blend of Wright and Voisin ideas. A. V. Roe's Triplane (*left*) is typical of new tractor propeller layouts.

Myer, Virginia, the *Flyer* which had been acquired by the United States Army. These demonstrations began from 3 September 1908, and people came in their thousands to see an aeroplane in flight for the first time. They were as thrilled and excited as the European spectators but tragically, within a matter of two weeks, the flights came to an end when the aircraft crashed. Orville was seriously injured, his passenger—Lt. Thomas E. Selfridge—was killed, the first man in the world to die in a powered aircraft accident. Subsequent investigation showed that a disintegrating propeller blade severed a bracing wire, allowing the tail unit to collapse. It is not in the nature of things that progress in any area is a continuous story of success.

Lessons were being learned in the very active European area, too, with the first use of ailerons for lateral control, the first powered flight being recorded in Britain by American S. F. Cody, and the first tentative 'hops' being achieved by Britain's A. V. Roe. And one of the lessons, learned by hard experience, was that overloaded engines overheat, lose power, and quickly opt out of the task of keeping their aircraft in the air. One of the prime requirements of a good aviator was the ability to keep an eye constantly appraising suitable emergency fields so that, when the engine overheated and called it a day, a quick and safe landing could be made in the chosen area.

It was all part of the sport of aviation, and didn't matter a great deal at a time when there was even enjoyment to be had in stripping, repairing and rebuilding a troublesome engine. It was likely to prove disconcerting, however, if aircraft were to be developed for the carriage of passengers, and unless engines of increased power became available there would be little scope for enlarging or reinforcing the "stick and string" airframe of the day.

Introduction of the rotary engine

Louis and Laurent Seguin, in France, began to investigate the problems associated with existing engines so that they could develop a new power plant which would satisfy the requirement of the day, as well as meet the needs of the future. Engines in use at that period were of two main types: in-line, which stemmed directly from the motor-car industry; and radial (the cylinders disposed radially around a circular crankcase), which had been developed as an aircraft power plant. The former were penalised at the outset by their origin, tending to be excessively

heavy and with the added disadvantage of needing a water cooling system, plus drag-inducing radiator. The radial engine relied upon air cooling, then far from effective because of bad cylinder design, and had large frontal area which held down the forward speed of the entire aircraft—a vicious circle of inefficiency.

The Seguins adopted a new engine configuration which could utilise air cooling, and consequent weight-saving, with cylinders and crankcase rotating around a fixed crankshaft; the aircraft's propeller was virtually one with this rotating mass. The resulting power plant, its cylinders rotating through the air, was adequately cooled, permitting the development of far more powerful engines. In addition, the flywheel torque of this revolving engine produced smooth power, even at small throttle openings. Despite the rather awesome appearance which a rotary engine presented on the first confrontation, it proved to be a most important interim power source, presenting airframe designers—for the first time—with as much power as was needed at the state of the art then existing.

One disadvantage was that, because the cylinders were rotating, a conventional carburettor set-up could not be used to supply the combustible mixture. Instead, a fuel/air mixture was admitted to the crankcase, entering the cylinders via ports in the cylinder walls. This raised lubrica-

tion complications, making essential the use of an oil not miscible with petrol. The resulting need for castor oil meant that engines had a characteristic smell which is associated nostalgically with rotary engines to this day. And because centrifugal force ensured that large quantities of oil passed straight through the engine, out of the exhaust ports and into the slipstream, both airframe and pilot were coated liberally. The oil consumption of a rotary engine could be from 25 to 50 per cent of the total fuel consumption, which meant that, in the long term, engines of this type would have proved totally unsuitable for long-range flight. Apart from that, when larger and more powerful engines were needed, the gyroscopic effect of the rotary

engine would have made handling the aircraft very difficult.

In those early years these factors were unimportant, and Gnome engines—as the Seguins named their creations—were to power many significant aircraft during the seven or eight years following their entry into service in 1909.

Elimination of natural barriers
This year was to see another important event in early aviation, the attainment of a milestone of great future significance. On 25 July, at approximately 05.17 hours, a frail-looking monoplane landed on the Northfall Meadow, close alongside Dover Castle, Kent. Piloted by Frenchman Louis Blériot, this man/machine combination

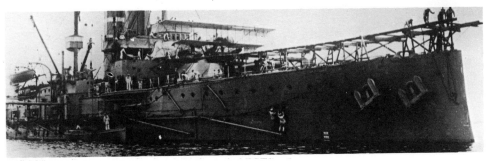

The historic moment of Blériot's arrival at Dover (*opposite top*) gave some idea of the potential of the aeroplane. In early 1910, Henri Fabre (*opposite bottom*) recorded the first flight from water of a powered aircraft. Later that same year Eugene Ely flew a Curtiss biplane off the cruiser USS *Birmingham* (*above*); in May 1912 Commander Sampson took off from the deck of the battleship HMS *Hibernia* (*left*), while it was under way, the first aviator to perform this feat.

had just completed the first crossing of the English Channel by a heavier-than-air craft. Blériot's Type XI monoplane which had made the crossing, in a time of 37 minutes, was powered by a three-cylinder Anzani engine of only 18·6 kW (25 hp). Despite the efficiency of Blériot's airframe, the engine almost succumbed to the contemporary problem of overheating, prevented from failure by a fortuitous shower of rain which cooled it sufficiently to complete the Channel crossing. Subsequently, Blériot monoplanes were to complete many important pioneering flights, but few could have caused such military concern as this first Channel crossing. For the first time it was clear that an island's geographic insularity was no longer adequate protection, relying solely upon its 'moat' of surrounding sea, policed by a strong navy.

Blériot monoplanes were to achieve some important first flights, including the first over the Alps (23 September 1910), the first London-Paris non-stop (12 April 1911), first official carriage of airmail in Britain (9 September 1911) and the United States (23 September 1911) and, inevitably, the first use of an aeroplane in war, on 22 October 1911.

Moves toward military aircraft

But regardless of the growing capability of the aeroplane, few military leaders could appreciate its potential other than for re-

connaissance purposes. This, despite the fact that, as early as 30 June 1910, Glenn Curtiss in America had demonstrated it was possible to drop weapons from an aircraft in flight. Subsequently, the first rifle was fired from an aeroplane on 20 August 1910, the first live bomb dropped from one on 7 January 1911, and later that same year a torpedo was launched from an aircraft for the first time.

Meanwhile, the potential of the aeroplane for naval use had not gone unnoticed. On 14 November 1910, Eugene Ely had flown a Curtiss biplane off the American Cruiser USS *Birmingham*: on 18 January 1911, he landed a similar aircraft on the Cruiser USS *Pennsylvania*. In Britain, Lt. C. R. Samson had made the first official flight from the battleship HMS *Africa*, on 10 January 1912. Four months later, during the Naval Review off Portland in May 1912, the then-promoted Commander Sampson was the first to fly an aeroplane off a ship under way, taking-off from the forecastle of HMS *Hibernia*.

But the lack of military acceptance was of little concern to the pioneers. Their aim, from the outset, had been to give to man the wings of a dove of peace. Orville Wright was to comment: "... we thought *(my brother and I)* that we were introducing into the world an invention which would make future wars practically impossible." A British pioneer, Claude Grahame-White, in a book written in as-

sociation with British aviation journalist Harry Harper, was to state "... the globe will be linked by flight, and nations so knit together that they will grow to be next-door neighbours."

The aim, from the outset; the belief, throughout these early years of development; the hope, so frequently expressed by the pioneers of aviation, was that the aeroplane would prove an instrument of peace in the world.

While people of all nations gazed at the aeroplane in wonder, as daring young men created those first flights which are the delight of today's historians, one nation was quietly building the biggest military air force in the world. When the First World War began, on 4 August 1914, Germany had approximately 280 aircraft available for use by its Army and Navy. Britain and France combined had slightly more aircraft in military service; Belgium had only 24. Significantly, however, the military potential of the aircraft in German use was, at that time, superior to that of the machines available to the Allies. In any event, it was of little importance to which of the combatant nations an aircraft belonged at that time. None were very lethal, except to their occupants. But this was only at the war's beginning. The aeroplane was to demonstrate, very quickly indeed, that it could—when properly used—prove a military weapon of the greatest importance.

THE FIRST WAR IN THE AIR

HAVING STATED that Britain entered the First World War with a not insignificant number of aircraft, it is necessary to explain why it could hardly be considered a potent military force. For a start, only a very small number of officers of the army could believe that the aeroplane had the capability of being used for wartime operations. There was, at the outset, no question of it being used for offensive purposes as it was unarmed. Let us be fair, though: its pilot carried a revolver, if he could gain access to it beneath the voluminous clothing worn to keep him reasonably warm in his open cockpit. His orders, on the initial Channel crossing to join the BEF, were to ram any Zeppelin airship which he might encounter *en route*, since this was the only hope he had of destroying such an aircraft. In one respect, his safety equipment was first class. The inflated rubber inner-tube around his waist promised security if a forced-landing in the Channel was dictated by engine-failure. He had no problems with carrying a parachute; he didn't have one. High authority believed the provision of such a device might encourage the pilot to abandon a damaged aircraft prematurely, instead of using his skill to get it back to base.

It was believed, however, that—providing the weather was fairly calm—it should be possible to use the aircraft as a reconnaissance platform for a trained observer. Reduced to the simplest terms, few had faith in a military aeroplane; and the aeroplanes available to the military were

hardly suitable for day-to-day, all-weather use.

There was a contradictory problem with stability. Because the only role envisaged for the aircraft was one of observation, it was assumed that the observation platform should be as stable as possible. Aircraft designers worked hard to provide their brain-children with this characteristic. Most successful was the young British designer Geoffrey de Havilland, whose B.E.2 biplane was a superb example of the inherently-stable aircraft. Flying a B.E.2B, Lt. Gilbert Mapplebeck, in company with Capt. (later Air Chief Marshal Sir) Philip Joubert de la Ferté in a Blériot XI monoplane, flew the first Royal Flying Corps (RFC) reconnaissance flight on 19 August 1914. The B.E.2 developed to its B.E.2C version was, perhaps, the most perfect observation aircraft of the First World War. Unfortunately, this very characteristic of stability was to prove a serious problem at a later stage.

Reconnaissance aircraft prove their value

At the war's beginning the German advance was breathtakingly fast. By the time it had been slowed to a halt on the banks of the River Marne, the new and untried appendages of the British and French armies had already demonstrated that aerial reconnaissance was of vital importance. Without its use in this initial stage of the First World War, the conflict might have ended in the first few weeks, with the German armies in Paris. This early use of

the new air arm had shown that not only was an observation aircraft able to report on enemy positions, the movement of reinforcements and supplies, and the sites chosen for munition dumps; it proved also, very quickly, that by spotting for batteries of field guns, and directing their fire, this hit-and-miss weapon had gained new importance. Communications which relied initially upon message-dropping and visual signalling were soon superseded by wireless telegraphy. And to make sure that an observer missed no small detail which might be of significance, aircraft were soon provided with cameras so that photographs could be studied and examined minutely for any information they might reveal.

But it should not be imagined that such developments were confined to the Allied air forces. The German High Command realised just as quickly the potential of these new eyes in the sky, and it became clear to the combatant nations that serious efforts must be made to prevent enemy reconnaissance aircraft from overflying home territory. This was especially true in areas where important troop movements were in progress, or where poker tactics were being used to hold a weak point in the line with minimal strength.

Military aircraft for different roles

From this need stemmed the entire family of military aeroplanes: firstly, arms for the reconnaissance aircraft; then escort fighters to accompany them over enemy

Following trials with the Royal Aircraft Factory B.E.2a, the B.E.2c evolved as a prime example of an inherently stable aircraft, which meant it could be flown hands-off. When 'gusted' off an even keel it could usually right itself.

The airship represented the first true achievement of the pioneers towards the realisation of practical flight. The balloon was a great sporting vehicle, but if flight was to become commercial, the vehicle must have a means of being steered from point to point and be able to carry a worthwhile payload. Airships such as that demonstrated by Roy Knabenshue in America (*right*) represented the first minimal advancement towards this aim in the early 1900s. The military potential of the developing airship was soon appreciated, and vessels such as the Italian semi-rigid P-type (*top*) were used for reconnaissance and bombing attacks in 1912. It was Count Ferdinand von Zeppelin in Germany, however, who succeeded in designing and building large Zeppelin airships (*below*) which, initially, were formidable weapons in WW1, and the most practical post-war airships.

The Bristol Fighter (*foreground*), known to WW1 pilots as the Brisfit, first flew on operations in April 1917. Its debut was disastrous, but the machine developed to excellence, remaining in RAF service until 1932. The Sopwith Pup, which went into service in 1916, was considered a superior aircraft by von Richthofen.

territory; fighters to take on enemy fighters; bombers to attack the bases from which an enemy's reconnaissance or fighter aircraft were deployed; bombers to attack factories building such aircraft, their engines and weapons. On the ground, steadily improving anti-aircraft guns were developed, to ensure that their high-velocity shells would keep observation aircraft at an altitude where they would be less able to carry out their task effectively.

The reconnaissance task was not limited to heavier-than-air craft; large numbers of gas-filled observation balloons were used initially by most combatant nations, until such time as they became sitting targets for fast aircraft armed with incendiary bullets. Germany, in particular, had developed a fleet of large Zeppelin airships, the majority of which were intended originally for use as naval reconnaissance vessels. Only as the war developed were they used instead as long-range strategic bombers.

These latter vessels were awe-inspiring weapons which seemed able to roam at will over British targets. Their size alone was frightening, with a length of more than 195 m (640 ft). But as defending

fighter aircraft gained the ability to climb above their operational height, and to attack them with incendiary bullets, they became far too vulnerable. When, on 5 August 1918, the pride of the German Naval Airship Division, the 211 m (692 ft 3 in) long L.70 was shot down over the North Sea, the use of airships as offensive weapons came to an end.

Development of fighter aircraft

The need to prevent an enemy's reconnaissance aircraft from having the freedom of the sky above your territory or lines meant that some way had to be devised to destroy the unwanted aircraft. Anti-aircraft guns were one of the weapons chosen for the task, but the likelihood of hitting a moving target some thousands of feet in the air was then a question of luck rather than judgement. They served to keep enemy aircraft flying high and, if the barrage was heavy enough, to keep them away from a particular area.

In the air, initial combat involved opposing pilots taking pot-shots at each other with pistols: their observers soon joined in, often using rather more accurate rifles, but there was an element of

medieval combat about these early encounters, with rather more than a hint of knightly conduct on both sides. It was not to last, because the need to prevent an enemy from getting back to base with important photographs or information was vital: so was the task of eliminating an aircraft that was directing the fall of heavy shells against your defensive positions.

So machine-guns were taken into the air, fired initially by the observer. This was practical for two-seat escort fighters, but was of little use to the pilot of a single-seat aircraft, who needed a machine-gun that was fixed rigidly to the aircraft and fired forwards. It was difficult to aim such a weapon, and if it jammed it was useless, unless within the pilot's reach. One solution was to mount the gun centrally, so that the pilot aimed his aircraft at the enemy, but there was still the problem of access to the gun for clearing stoppages and, in the case of a Lewis gun, of reloading with new drums of ammunition. The ideal position was on the upper fuselage, directly forward of the pilot's windscreen, but this meant that the stream of bullets would have to pass through the disc of the rotating propeller.

French pilot Roland Garros and French aircraft designer Raymond Saulnier mounted a machine-gun in the ideal position on a Morane-Saulnier single-seat fighter, attaching steel deflector plates to the backs of the propeller blades to deflect any bullets which would otherwise splinter the wooden blades. Garros was able to demonstrate quickly the effectiveness of such a weapon, destroying at least three enemy aircraft before force-landing in enemy territory.

The significance of the machine-gun and deflector plates was appreciated quickly by the Germans who inspected the captured aircraft. Initially they wanted to copy this crude system, but designers Leinberger and Lübbe of the Fokker Company devised an interrupter gear which timed the discharge of bullets from a forward-mounted machine-gun so that they would pass between the propeller blades. The resulting combination of highly manoeuvrable Fokker monoplanes with forward-firing machine-guns proved a serious problem to the Allies.

The Royal Flying Corps, in particular, found itself at a grave disadvantage. The inherently stable B.E.2c was useless

Britain's Sopwith Snipe (*above*) was one of the best fighter-scouts of WW1. When the United States became involved they had no significant combat aircraft, and had to rely on supplies from their Allies. They built, however, an excellent trainer in the JN series, and a JN-4 is shown (*top left*). Typical of fighter-scouts used by the Americans in France is the French Nieuport 28C-1 (*far left*). The Fokker Dr.1 triplane (*below*) is one of the best remembered German aircraft, flown by Manfred von Richthofen, but the Fokker D.VII (*left*) is regarded as one of the great warplanes of all time; armistice terms demanded that all were surrendered to the Allies.

The Zeppelin Staaken R.VI (*below*) was one of Germany's so-called Giant bombers, spanning 44·21 m (138 ft 5½ in), which had sufficient range to carry its load of eighteen 100 kg bombs to attack not only targets on the Eastern and Western Fronts, but to the heart of England's capital city. Maximum take-off weight of the R.VI was 11,460 kg (25,265 lb), equalling the take-off weight of about sixteen Avro 504Ks, (*bottom*). This superb training aircraft has a unique place in aviation history, because the foundation of modern flying training was evolved with this aircraft in the hands of instructors of the RFC's School of Special Flying, men who used the techniques of flying training developed by Major R. R. Smith-Barry. But even this diminutive trainer had started life as a reconnaissance aircraft, and had first won its spurs bombing Zeppelin sheds in Germany. When, on 21 November 1914, Royal Naval Air Service Avro 504s recorded the first ever strategic bombing attack by a formation of aircraft, each carried the diminutive load of four 20lb bombs.

when attacked, unable to out-manoeuvre the enemy and, because the observer who was armed with the machine-gun was restricted in his field of fire by the wings, their struts and bracing wires, unable to fight back effectively. Within no time at all, the observation aircraft of the Allies were being driven from the sky, unless accompanied by a mass of escorting fighters. This was the beginning of the period of dominance by the German air force known as the 'Fokker Scourge', lasting from October 1915 until May of the following year.

For the Allies it was essential to evolve rapidly a new family of very manoeuvrable and hard-hitting fighter aircraft and, in the main, the RFC's requirements were met by the Royal Aircraft Factory at Farn-borough, Hampshire. The British Admiralty followed a different line of procurement, relying upon private manufacturers, and some of their aircraft—such as the Sopwith Pup—were adopted also by the RFC. The French aircraft industry followed similar lines of development, as involvement in the same theatres of war brought identical experience. This nation's industry was to benefit from the fact that it had been well established prior to the war, enabling it not only to produce excellent aircraft for the needs of its own armed forces, but having also adequate productive capacity to build aircraft in quantity for its Allies. This was to be of considerable importance in April 1917 when the United States entered the war, for although that nation's armed forces possessed some 250 aircraft, none were more effective than the simplest training aircraft of the belligerent nations. At the end of the Second World War about seventy-five per cent of United States military aircraft operating at the Western Front had been supplied from French or British manufacturing sources.

The development of bomber aircraft
Germany's early reliance upon the Zeppelin airships to fulfil the long-range strategic bombing requirement had meant reduced priority for the development of heavier-than-air craft to carry out both tactical and strategic bombing attacks. The Allies, on the other hand, had never envisaged the deployment of airships in such a role, both Britain and France

Germany's A.E.G. G.IV (*right*) was another of the significant bomber aircraft that evolved during WW1. Its range proved inadequate and the majority were used for short-range tactical missions. The Vickers Vimy (*below*) was intended as a strategic bomber to attack industrial targets in Germany. It was too late to see operational service in WW1, but made many important post-war flights, including the first heavier-than-air North Atlantic crossing.

confining the activities of such aircraft to maritime patrol, in the North Sea and Mediterranean respectively. Both nations found them to be valuable anti-submarine weapons, not by taking direct action themselves, but by calling upon other naval forces to deal with these vessels.

As a result, the Allies were rather quicker to become involved in the development of suitable aeroplanes to satisfy the tactical or strategic role. Early attacks against the Zeppelin sheds were made by fighter aircraft carrying small bombs, but gradually, as the importance of attacks against military targets and supply bases and factories became apparent, manufacturers in Britain and France began to embark on the development of bomber aircraft.

One of the most important early aircraft to enter service with the RFC in the bomber capacity was the D.H.4 day bomber, hitting the enemy hard under the operational guidance of the RAF's legendary father-figure, Hugh Trenchard. By 1917 both the RFC and the German air force were making use of specially-developed heavy bombers, Britain using the Handley Page 0/100 and F.E.2b.

Germany had evolved the Gotha heavy bomber and Zeppelin-Staaken series of giant bombers. When the former made daylight attacks on London in June and July 1917, appearing to range freely over the capital without any sign of opposition, the resulting public outcry ensured that the subject of this alarming gap in Britain's defences was debated in Parliament and, following enquiry and investigation, resulted in the creation of the independent Royal Air Force on 1 April 1918.

First Chief of the Air Staff was Major-General Sir Hugh (later Lord) Trenchard, and when he found difficulty in working with the Secretary of State for Air, he resigned as Chief of the Air Staff and returned to France to create the Independent Air Force in June 1918. As a firm believer in the capability of air power, Trenchard was the ideal man to establish the Independent Force, comprising initially day bombers transferred from the RAF, plus Handley Page 0/400s borrowed from the former Royal Naval Air Service, then integrated into the RAF. In the closing stages of the war even bigger bombers were being developed by British manufacturers, including the Vickers Vimy and Handley Page V/1500. Both were completed too late to be used on wartime operations.

When the war ended, on 11 November 1918, all of the nations involved had gained an appreciation of the capability of air power. In particular, Hugh Trenchard in Britain, William ('Billy') Mitchell of the US Army Air Service and Giulio Douhet of the Italian Air Force had become dedicated protagonists of air power, convinced that a nation which possessed a potent air force could dominate the army and navy of an aggressor. We shall see how, in the inter-war years, these beliefs helped to shape the air forces which were to become involved in the Second World War.

THE CONQUEST OF THE GLOBE

THERE STILL EXISTS a widespread belief that wartime utilisation of aircraft in a combat or offensive role had brought about complete emancipation of the aeroplane. In fact, no such thing had happened. In the main, an airframe still relied upon a mass of struts and bracing wires to maintain its rigidity. The real change had come in the development of far more powerful engines: the 37·3–74·6 kW (50 to 100 hp) power plants with which the various nations had gone to war, had been replaced by engines that were no less reliable, and which had outputs ranging from 149–224 kW (200 to 300 hp).

Thus, the constant cry of the aircraft designer for more power had been met. But instead of developing 'clean' aircraft, free from drag-inducing struts and bracing wires, designers had tended to follow their noses, building bigger, better equipped, machines that relied upon the increased power of their engines to drag them through the air. The external appearance of a biplane of 1918 tended to differ little, except in size, from that produced by the same company in the early days of the war.

The growing capability of aircraft during the war was clearly recognised by those interested in the post-war development of civil air services. As early as 5 October 1916, George Holt Thomas in Britain had registered a company named Aircraft Transport and Travel Ltd.; shortly afterwards, in France, Pierre Latécoère was planning how he might link his native country with Morocco. His ultimate dream was an air service for passengers, cargo and mail, spanning the South Atlantic to South America.

They, and others like them, had failed to appreciate that considerable development of specialised aircraft was necessary before such air services became routine. They had also overlooked the fact that the potential air traveller was not yet ready to accept the aeroplane as the best means of getting from A to B. The majority of people who, in those early post-war years, would have the need to travel for business or pleasure, were still under the impression that flying was for heroes, certainly not for the mere man in the street.

The first post-war civil airline services

On 25 August 1919, Aircraft Transport and Travel inaugurated the first post-war scheduled civil air service between London and Paris. This was followed first by Handley Page Transport and then by S. Instone and Co., both operating services over the same route. France had also started civil operations, recording the first scheduled international passenger service between Paris and Brussels, on 22 March 1919. Compagnie des Messageries Aériennes and Compagnie des Grands Express Aériens also began services between London and Paris, with the result that too many aircraft were chasing a non-existent queue of passengers. Within a few years the competing private companies operating these and other European services found themselves in grave financial difficulties, leading to the formation of national airlines such as Air France, Deutsche Lufthansa, Imperial Airways, KLM and Sabena.

With the aircraft that were available to the early airlines in the immediate post-war years, flying could be considered uncomfortable rather than unsafe. The only machines then obtainable were ex-military, with limited accommodation adapted for the carriage of passengers. What had been the gunner's position in a D.H.4 day-bomber, for example, could be provided with seats for two passengers, crammed face-to-face in the narrow fuselage, beneath a celluloid-windowed fuselage lid. Ventilation just happened; heating could be provided by heavy clothing, rugs and a hot-water bottle. A pair of household wooden steps was provided to make it easy to board the aircraft. And the single fare could cost you about £6 from London to Paris. For the current equivalent sterling value one could fly from London to New York today.

So, travel by air was expensive and unpopular. Only the wealthy or the brave took to the air. For them it was probably a good investment, for the passengers of an aircraft which had made one or more forced landings would have acquired a fund of exciting anecdotes which would ensure their selection as dinner guests for months ahead. Believe it or not, one of Aircraft Transport and Travel's 'airliners' made a record 22 forced landings on a single 'flight' between London and Paris.

The beginning of the great flights

Some catalyst was needed, powerful enough and widely reported, which would convince the 'man in the street' that he, too, could fly as a passenger. In Britain, the *Daily Mail* newspaper had, from the date of the first powered flight in Europe, done much to sponsor aviation progress

The Swallow (*above*) is typical of the open-cockpit biplanes with which such men as Charles Lindbergh first pioneered the airmail routes of North America.

The Vickers Vimy (*below*) was the type used by Alcock and Brown to record the first historic non-stop west–east crossing of the North Atlantic; the Ryan Monoplane *Spirit of St. Louis* (*bottom*) carried Charles Lindbergh on the first great New York–Paris flight, an epic solo achievement. The airship R.100 (*right*), designed by Barnes N. Wallis (later Sir), also flew the North Atlantic, to and from Canada in the Summer of 1930. The Vimy's flight was made without the aid of any sophisticated navigational devices; yet inertial guidance systems of modern airliners provide pin-point landfall at transatlantic ranges. Lindbergh's achievement was one of indomitable courage and skilful navigation, his primary problem to keep awake for almost 34 hours of flight. The R.100, with 44 people on board, made its double Atlantic crossing with such ease that it seemed the future of long-range transport could be satisfied by such aircraft. It was wishful thinking: a number of fatal accidents soon showed that airships were not the answer.

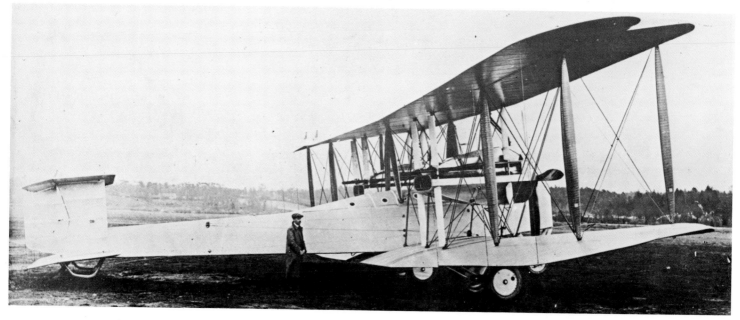

by the promise of substantial prizes for specific achievements. There had been, for example, £1,000 for the first cross-Channel flight, £10,000 for the first London–Manchester flight, and £10,000 for the winner of the first 'Round Britain' air race. All of these prizes had been won before the war and, so far as the public was concerned, long forgotten.

The *Daily Mail* had offered another £10,000 prize, for the first crossing of the North Atlantic, and this was won by Captain John Alcock and Lt. Arthur Whitten Brown who flew from St. John's, Newfoundland to Clifden, County Galway, Ireland (Eire) on 14–15 June 1919. Their mount was a specially-prepared Vickers Vimy, which it will be recalled had been developed as a long-range strategic bomber late in the war. This was the first of the great achievements that were, over a period of time, to convince the non-flying public that a new, safe method of fast travel was developing rapidly.

Less than six months after Alcock and Brown's North Atlantic crossing the Australian brothers Captain Ross and Lt. Keith Smith set off to make the first flight between England and Australia. They, too, used a specially prepared Vimy, completing the 18,175 km (11,294 miles) flight between 12 November and 10 December 1919, to win a £10,000 prize offered by the government of Australia.

From that moment on, the pace of progress got faster and faster. The first flight

across Australia had been accomplished between 16 November to 12 December 1919; the first flight between Britain and South Africa from 4 February to 20 March 1920; the first non-stop crossing of the United States on 2–3 May 1923; the first round-the-world flight was completed between 6 April and 28 September 1924; and the first aeroplane flight over the North Pole on 9 May 1926.

All of these flights gained world headlines, and brought some measure of confidence in the aeroplane. But something was still needed to capture the hearts and imagination of ordinary people all over the world. Then, at 07.52 hrs on 20 May 1927, a small (14 m; 46 ft span) single-engined monoplane literally staggered off a rain-soaked field at Long Island, New York. Heavily laden with fuel, it only just cleared obstructions at the end of the field and climbed slowly, almost reluctantly, into lowering skies. The pilot, little-known except to his colleagues involved in carrying the US Air Mail, headed his aircraft out over the Atlantic, aiming for the diminutive target of Le Bourget airport, Paris. Thirty-three hours 39 min later, in the glare of car headlights and before an almost unbelievable crowd of cheering

people, the little Ryan monoplane *Spirit of St. Louis* came in to land at Le Bourget. Never again could its pilot claim anonymity, for this was the legendary Charles Lindbergh. His flight, the first solo non-stop crossing of the North Atlantic, was that which more than any other enchanted the peoples of the world. If, they argued, one man in a small aeroplane with only one engine could fly safely from New York to Paris—a distance of 5,810 km (3,610 miles)—then air travel must be safe for anyone wanting to travel over domestic and short-range intercontinental services. This single achievement gave a tremendous fillip to air services everywhere, and especially to domestic services in the United States.

On the subject of achievements, during the two years which followed Charles Lindbergh's Atlantic crossing, Costes and Le Brix made the first flight across the South Atlantic; 'Bert' Hinkler flew solo from England to Australia; Kingsford Smith and Ulm with a two-man crew achieved the first trans-Pacific flight; Sqdn. Ldr. Jones Williams and Flt. Lt. Jenkins of the RAF flew non-stop from England to India. In August 1929, the German *Graf Zeppelin* made a round-the-world flight in just 3 weeks.

Developments in lighter-than-air craft

The post-war development of airships had seemed to offer an important means of travel on long-distance routes. When, be-

tween 2 and 6 July and 10 and 13 July 1919 the British airship R-34 flew to Canada and back to accomplish the first airship crossing and the first two-way crossing of the North Atlantic, the protagonists of lighter-than-air craft were convinced that there was immense potential for cruise-liner type services over long ranges.

Germany, forbidden to build aircraft by the terms of the Versailles Treaty, attempted to resuscitate the airship service between Berlin and Friedrichshafen which had operated so successfully pre-war, but this was soon stopped by the Allied Control Commission. Count von Zeppelin had died before the war's end and his associate from the early days, Dr. Hugo Eckner, had taken over control of the company. They were difficult times, but Dr. Eckner ensured the continuance of the company by building the LZ.126 by way of reparations to the US. This ship, named the USS *Los Angeles*, was an immense success in US Navy Service, accumulating well over 5,000 flight hours before being scrapped finally in 1939.

The Zeppelin company went on to build the highly successful *Graf Zeppelin*, first flown on 18 September 1928, and subsequently the world's largest airship, the LZ.129 *Hindenburg*, which was 245 m (803·81 ft) in length with a maximum diameter of 41 m (134·5 ft).

Britain also built two large airships for civil air services, the R.100, designed for

the Airship Guarantee Company by a team under the leadership of Barnes Wallis (later Sir), and the R.101, designed and built at the Air Ministry's Royal Airship Works at Cardington, Bedfordshire. Between 29 July and 16 August 1930, the R.100 flew to Canada and back on a proving flight which was highly successful. The R.101, on the contrary, crashed at Beauvais, France, on its proving flight to India, killing 48 of its 54 occupants. This event brought to an end the development of British airships, and the R.100 was scrapped.

In America both the Army and Navy operated a number of airships, the latter having a large quantity of non-rigid 'ships in service at various times. In addition, the US Navy operated the German-built USS *Los Angeles*, acquiring subsequently two more large rigid vessels, the USS *Akron* and USS *Macon*. When both these latter 'ships were lost at sea, in 1933 and 1935 respectively, the Navy's rigid airship programme was brought to an end.

In Germany, the *Graf Zeppelin* was going from success to success: it seemed that a vessel had been designed and built which could provide the long-range civil services which it was believed was within the capability of such aircraft. By the time this airship was scrapped, in 1940, it had accumulated 17,178 flying hours, made—among nearly 600 flights—140 Atlantic crossings, and had carried 13,100 passengers. The Zeppelin company had

The Ford Trimotor, or 'Tin Goose' as it was known popularly, had been produced originally in the 1920s. It utilised the corrugated metal skin which had been pioneered by Hugo Junkers in Germany, hence its nickname. Junkers later produced a tri-motor monoplane, but of cantilever low-wing configuration.

a cruising speed of only 160 km/h (100 mph)—so that Anthony Fokker described them as having built-in headwinds—these majestic aeroplanes gained such a reputation for safety and comfort that, in the 1930s, they carried more passengers between London and the Continent of Europe than all other airlines combined. E and W versions of the H.P.42 carried 24 and 38 passengers respectively, the latter serving on the short-haul European routes. They accommodated the flight crew within the fuselage on a flight deck for the first time: it was finally understood that the pilot and his crew would be able to work far more efficiently under such conditions than if they were frozen to the marrow and exposed in an open cockpit to the worst the weather could offer.

Even greater changes were coming, in America, where domestic air routes had expanded rapidly following the stimulus of Lindbergh's Atlantic flight. They had a good basis on which to develop, for the US Air Mail Service had linked major towns across the nation with navigational beacons, airfields and other facilities. All that was needed was a new generation of specially-designed transport aircraft.

On 8 February 1933 a very significant prototype aircraft made its first flight: the Boeing Model 247, which set entirely new standards. A low-wing monoplane of all-metal construction, powered by two 410 kW (550 hp) Pratt & Whitney air-cooled radial engines, it introduced several important new ideas that would add considerably to the performance of aircraft the world over. These included retractable landing gear, variable-pitch propellers, control surface trim tabs, de-icing equipment and an automatic pilot. It was the first twin-engined aircraft capable of climbing with a full load on the power of one engine, a fact which added considerably to safety in the critical areas of take-off and landing.

When the Model 247 was introduced into service by United Air Lines (UAL), a passenger could travel coast-to-coast across America in less than 20 hours, and this high-speed service sparked off a spate of development as a result of which the US manufacturers gained a lead in the production of civil transport aircraft which they have managed to retain to this day.

Other US airlines, losing revenue to

every reason to believe that, as a result of their experience with the *Graf Zeppelin*, the subsequent *Hindenburg* would recoup the company's fortunes, and that airline operators would want to acquire similar craft to inaugurate prestigious long-range services. It was not to be. Because supplies of non-inflammable helium could not be obtained to inflate the *Hindenburg*, her gas cells had been filled instead with hydrogen. When the giant airship approached the mooring mast at Lakehurst, New Jersey, on 6 May 1939, static electricity ignited venting gas and, within seconds, the Hindenburg collapsed in a blazing mass. By a miracle, 62 of the 97 people on board escaped with their lives, but this disaster was the last straw. Commercial airship development came to an end.

Start of the flying clubs
Just a couple of years before Lindbergh's North Atlantic flight, an important aircraft had been designed and built by Geoffrey de Havilland in the United Kingdom. This was the de Havilland Moth, the prototype of which flew for the first time on 22 February 1925. A lightweight biplane,

powered by a four-cylinder in-line engine, it was the aircraft chosen to start the government-sponsored British Flying Club Movement. It was built subsequently in America, Australia, Canada, Finland, France and Norway, and is regarded generally as being responsible for the start of the worldwide flying club movement.

The de Havilland Moth was one link in the chain which made people aware of the potential of air travel. Subsequent achievements by ordinary people flying Moths added new links to the chain, including the first solo flight from England to Australia by a woman, accomplished by Amy Johnson between 5–14 May 1930. (And such is the affection for the Moth that in early 1978, Flight Lieutenant David Cyster flew one from Darwin to London to commemorate the 50th anniversary of Hinkler's solo flight to Australia in 1928.)

New airliners enter service
Next came another link, in 1931, when Britain's Imperial Airways introduced a fleet of Handley Page H.P.42/45 four-engined biplane airliners. Despite having

DEVELOPMENTS IN PASSENGER COMFORT

The first post-war civil aircraft were somewhat casual conversions of machines which had been used by the air forces during WW1. The austere accommodation available in the immediate post-war years did little to enthuse travellers to take to the air, and it was not until purpose-built airliners began to enter service that the passenger was able to find a degree of comfort. The Argosy airliners of Imperial Airways in 1927 had a steward to serve a buffet lunch to the 18 passengers on its *Silver Wing* service (*right*). Very different is the interior of a modern wide-body jet airliner such as the McDonnell Douglas DC-10 (*below*), which has accommodation for a maximum of 380 passengers in air-conditioned luxury. The original 'Jumbo jet', Boeing's Model 747, can carry as many as 500 passengers.

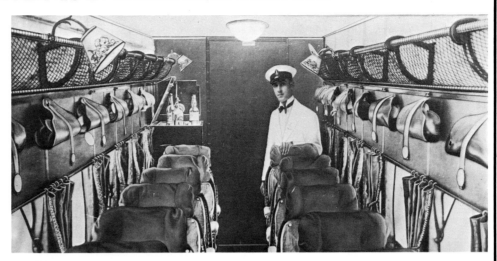

The Handley Page W9 *Hampstead* (*below*) was developed from the earlier W8b 12-passenger airliner. It differed by having three engines, instead of two, providing a higher cruising speed, and could seat 14 passengers in wicker chairs.

In the early 1930s this scene at Croydon Airport gave immense pride to those who worked hard to put civil aviation on a sound footing in the UK. This Handley Page H.P.42W *Horatius* of Imperial Airways was one of four Croydon-based 42Ws which linked London with Europe. But the Boeing Model 247 (*right*), a contemporary, made these reliable biplanes look as if they had originated in another age.

UAL, decided to approach the Douglas Company to produce a competing aircraft. The resulting DC-2 proved to be even more comfortable than the 247, carried four more passengers, was faster, and introduced wing trailing-edge flaps which improved take-off and landing performance. From the DC-2 Douglas evolved a wider-fuselage DST (Douglas Sleeper Transport), followed by one of the most famous aircraft in the history of civil aviation, the 21-seat DC-3. In the period 1939–1940, when some 80 per cent of civil transports used by America's domestic airlines were DC-3s, a 100 per cent safety record was maintained. As this is written, in 1978, large numbers of these remarkable aircraft remain in service with airlines around the world.

Development of intercontinental routes

With the establishment of domestic routes in Europe and North America, airlines began to investigate the possibility of inaugurating intercontinental services over long ranges. Not surprisingly, most countries decided to use for such services aircraft which could operate from water: after all, 70 per cent of the Earth's surface

The Douglas C-47 (*left*) is a military variant of the DC-3. Both earned a unique place in aviation history, primarily because of their reliability. The contemporary German Junkers Ju 52/3m (*bottom left*) gained equal respect; the name *Tante Ju* bestowed by Luftwaffe pilots showed their trust in this multi-purpose transport aircraft.

is covered with water, and the development of flying-boats appeared to make good sense. Thus, when Britain decided to introduce the Empire Air Mail Scheme in late 1934, which meant that Imperial Airways would carry all mail for Commonwealth countries, the airline ordered a fleet of four-engined flying-boats from Short Brothers. Designated S.23, the first of these, named *Canopus*, made its first revenue flight on 30 October 1936: by mid-1938 S.23s were operating a through service from Southampton to Sydney.

America looked out across the vast reaches of the Pacific Ocean, planning a route via island stepping stones. Bases were therefore prepared on Wake Island and Guam—both US territory—to permit a route from San Francisco via Honolulu, Wake and Guam to Manila, with the first stage––to Honolulu—being the longest (3,853 km; 2,394 miles). The Martin Company built three four-engined flying-boats for this service, to the specification of Pan American Airways, and the first of these M-130 boats, the *China Clipper*, inaugurated the first trans-Pacific mail service on 22 November 1935. It was not until 21 October 1936 that fare-paying passengers were first carried.

France and Germany were both interested in developing a route across the South Atlantic. France began by establishing a service between Toulouse and Dakar, but it was 1928 before it was possible to open a route between Toulouse and Buenos Aires. This was not, however, a full air route, the ocean sector being operated by ships. It was not until 12 May 1930 that legendary French pilot Jean Mermoz took off from Senegal in the Latécoère seaplane *Comte de La Vaulx* to make the first direct crossing to Natal. More suitable aircraft were needed before a regular service could be established, and three-engined Couzinet 71 flying-boats began a regular South Atlantic mail service on 28 May 1934. But passengers were not carried over this route until after the Second World War.

Germany, initially, opted to use the *Graf Zeppelin* across the South Atlantic, the first trial flight from Friedrichshafen to Rio de Janeiro beginning on 18 May 1930. Proving successful, airship services between Germany and Recife, Brazil, were inaugurated on 20 March 1932 and continued at an average of one return trip per month into 1936. The alternative German plan was to use Dornier flying-boats to link Africa and South America, with landplanes providing the service over the remainder of the route. And to ensure that the flying-boats could take off with maximum fuel and full payload, a method of catapulting these aircraft off depot ships was adopted, enabling regular air mail services to begin on 7 February 1934. Subsequently, improved Dornier Do 26s were able to make a direct, unassisted crossing, and when the Second World War brought the service to an end, well over 300 crossings had been completed by various Dornier flying-boats.

Conquest of the North Atlantic

What about the North Atlantic? A good question, for it seems strange that this, the first ocean to be conquered by both airship and aeroplane, should not have been the first to have regular air services linking the Old and New World.

It was not for want of enthusiasm that the North Atlantic was the last of the oceans to be conquered by air, for the commercial potential was apparent to all. Distance, unreliable weather and strong prevailing westerly winds conspired to make such a service impossible until reliable aircraft of long-range capability were available for the task.

Not until the late 1930s was the time considered right, and the interested nations began experimental flights. France utilised a six-engined flying-boat, the Latécoère 521, which made its first crossing to New York, via Lisbon and the Azores, in August 1938. Germany experimented with the depot ship technique which had been used on the South Atlantic route, several crossings being made by this method in 1936 and 1937 by Dornier Do 18 flying-boats and Blohm und Voss Ha 139 seaplanes. And in 1938 a specially-prepared Focke-Wulf Fw 200 Condor landplane made a successful Berlin-New York and return flight, pointing the way to the future.

Interim British solutions included the Short-Mayo composite, the S.21 *Maia* flying-boat taking off with the S.20 *Mercury* seaplane carried pick-a-back. The *Mercury* could thus be air-launched with a maximum fuel load and payload, which made it impossible for it to get into the air without assistance. On 20–21 July 1938 *Mercury* made the first commercial crossing of the North Atlantic by a heavier-

Once upon a time flying-boats dominated the long-range air travel scene. This intentionally begins like a child's fairy story because there was a romantic and almost magical aura about these great vessels. Open waterways used for take-off meant there was no serious restriction to the length of run, so flying-boats were usually much bigger than landplanes of the same era. The Boeing 314 (*above*) provided the first regular transatlantic services. The Sikorsky S-42 (*left*) surveyed both Atlantic and Pacific; while the Grumman Goose (*below*) operates both from land and water, making it a true amphibian.

than-air craft, flying non-stop from Foynes to Montreal. It was, however, an impractical solution, and proved to be of no commercial use. Britain experimented also with the use of Short C-class flying-boats which were air refuelled to maximum capacity by Handley Page Harrow tankers after take-off, and completed successfully a series of trial flights which terminated on 30 September 1939, after Britain had become involved in the Second World War.

It remained for America's Pan American Airways — which had been making experimental flights simultaneously with those of Imperial Airways—to inaugurate the first regular transatlantic mail service on 20 May 1939. Finally, on 8 July 1939, Pan Am's Boeing 314 *Yankee Clipper* flying-boat carried 17 passengers and the mail on the inaugural northern route transatlantic service.

It had taken so long to achieve success on this, the most difficult ocean route in the world, it seems unjust that the achievement was overshadowed and overlooked as a result of the gathering war clouds in Europe. By the end of the Second World War, a complete new generation of civil airliners was in prospect.

THE NEW AIRBORNE ARMIES

WITH THE SIGNING of the Versailles Treaty the 'war to end wars' was over. The cost in human lives was almost unbelievable; the cost in monetary terms was to bring enormous problems to all the nations which had been involved. Germany was forbidden to build or operate military aircraft; the other nations, believing that the four years of madness would have taught an unforgettable lesson, reduced their armed forces to a minimum.

Apart from the reductions in manpower and the disposal of surplus equipment, it meant that for some years ahead air forces would have to make do with the types of aircraft that had equipped their squadrons at the war's end. For aircraft manufacturers it was a bleak prospect as contracts for thousands of machines were cancelled. To stay in business many had to move into different fields of manufacture, often turning to the production of furniture and other domestic goods of which their national home markets had been starved during the war. As we have seen, the world was not then ready for a large civil aviation industry and, in consequence, there was no demand for the development of new civil aircraft. Practically the only

aviation work available was the conversion of wartime aircraft for civil use, and even this requirement was very limited.

National developments

With the end of the war, Hugh Trenchard was reappointed Chief of the Air Staff in 1919. He took with him to the Air Ministry his profound belief in strategic air power and a determination to ensure that before he relinquished the reins he would build the foundation of an air force that could deal with any eventuality.

The United States Army Air Service had ended the war with a rapidly growing force. In immediate tactical command of its front line squadrons at the Western Front was Colonel William ('Billy') Mitchell, a disciple of Trenchard. After a period with the Army of Occupation, he returned to America to find that the Air Service had been reduced to a mere shadow of its wartime strength. Appointed Assistant Chief of the USAAS, Mitchell, too, was determined to bring about changes, convinced of the doctrine of strategic air power, as well as of the need to make the Air Service an independent force, free of Army control.

There was yet another prophet of air power, the Italian General Giulio Douhet, who in 1921 published a treatise *The Command of the Air*, expressing his convictions that stategic air power should be the dominant feature of military planning, since both armies and navies would eventually become subservient to air power.

France, which with Belgium had been the main board on which the battles of the First World War had been played, was thinking primarily in terms of defence. The immense and costly fortifications called the Maginot Line were constructed, in the firm belief that it would prove more than adequate to prevent another invasion from Germany.

Japan had no significant aircraft industry until the early 1920s, and prior to that time only small numbers of aeroplanes of European design had been built under licence. Realising that her small Army and Navy air forces needed practical instruction in military aviation, a service mission was invited from France in 1919 to provide essential education for the Army air force in aerial combat, gunnery, reconnaissance and bombing techniques. This was so successful that, in 1921, the Japan-

These between-wars military aircraft have a disparity in size, but both played a significant role in RAF training. The de Havilland Tiger Moth primary trainer (*bottom left*) remained in service for 15 years. The Vickers Virginia (*below*) was an important night bomber, teaching skills invaluable in WW2, when RAF Bomber Command was primarily a night force.

ese Navy invited a similar mission from Britain. This also proved of great importance, providing technical instruction which covered subjects from the basics of flight control to aerial photography and the use of torpedo-launching aircraft. The lessons were well learned and in just 20 years the Japanese had created formidable air forces.

In Russia, after the holocaust of the Communist Revolution, a new and powerful air force was created gradually. Much assistance in the later development of the Red Air Force came from German sources, in return for facilities at Lipezk, in Russia, where for eight years the new Luftwaffe was trained in secret.

Trenchard plans the future RAF
A most important event in British military aviation came in 1919, with the publication in December of an official document which has found its way into history as Trenchard's White Paper. In this, the Chief of Air Staff advocated the retention of an independent air force, with small units to be trained especially for co-

operation with the Navy and Army. This led to the creation at a later date of the Fleet Air Arm and Army Air Corps. But the most important section of this document was that which detailed Trenchard's proposals for the training of a Royal Air Force which, though small, could be expanded as needed in a time of national crisis. Furthermore, this high quality and careful training, allied to the practical experience which the air force gained while helping to maintain law and order, or as a result of involvement in the small-scale wars and insurrections which persisted almost continuously between the First and Second World Wars, was to provide an elite corps of airmen, both in the air and on the ground. When the real challenge came, in 1939, they were ready for it.

The Importance of the Schneider Trophy
The surplus of aircraft which the RAF inherited at the end of the First World War meant that, in the main, they had to soldier on into the early 1930s before any significant new machines came their way. When they materialised, some bore the

imprint of the influence on aircraft and engine design which had resulted from the Schneider Trophy Contests initiated by Jacques Schneider, in France, in late 1912. Schneider's original aim had been to speed the development of aircraft which could operate from water, believing that the future of air transport was linked closely with water-borne aircraft, or hyroaeroplanes as they were then known. But these international contests evolved into air races between high speed seaplanes, most of which had just about sufficient room within their streamlined fuselage to accommodate a pilot.

In the development of these aircraft, designers learned a great deal about building sleek monoplane—and biplane—structures, the importance of streamlining and the significance of an aircraft's shape in keeping drag to a minimum. At the same time, specialist designers evolved far more powerful engines. These were, of course, short life racing engines, but the experience they gained in building, testing and operating such machines led to new power plants of

New generations of fighter aircraft were developed between the wars. The Boeing P-26 of the US (*left*) and the biplane built by Emile Dewoitine in Switzerland (*bottom left*) had similar bluff lines, being built around radial engines. R. J. Mitchell's Supermarine S 6B (*below*) had the streamlined form that later graced the Spitfire.

greater reliability and much improved power/weight ratio. The Curtiss D-12 engine and Curtiss/Reed propeller developed in America was one of these remarkable power plants of the early 1920s, a small-diameter propeller allowing the construction of an engine which needed no reduction-gear drive to ensure that the propeller tips did not exceed a certain critical speed. This simplification not only reduced the overall weight of the engine, but meant that power needed normally to drive the reduction gearing was available instead for propulsion. In the UK, the Rolls-Royce R (racing) engine of 1,752 kW (2,350 hp) which speeded the Supermarine S 6B seaplane to victory in 1931, finally winning the Schneider Trophy outright for Britain, was developed initially into a new 746 kW (1,000 hp) military power plant called the Merlin. The Supermarine S.4, S.5 and S.6 series of racing seaplanes designed by R. J. Mitchell led him to the creation of the famous monoplane eight-gun Spitfire fighter, which utilised the Merlin engine as its power plant. In aviation, as in the motor car industry, the spur of competition improved not only the capability of

the vehicle, but also its mechanical efficiency and reliability.

Development of air forces

In America, Billy Mitchell campaigned ceaselessly for an independent air force, demonstrated (though under unrealistic conditions) that aircraft had the capability of sinking capital ships, and following persistent campaigning and criticism of senior command was court martialled, and sentenced to five years suspension from duty. Instead, he resigned from the service so that he could continue to use every means at his disposal to influence the creation of the kind of air force which he was certain the United States needed.

Despite Mitchell's efforts, America retained Army and Navy air forces, the former service operating primarily for army co-operation until the provision of long-range bombers and defensive fighters in the 1930s brought a change of policy. In the inter-war period the US Navy built six aircraft carriers and procured a series of ship-board aircraft, mostly with dive-bombing capability. When, in 1926, a navy squadron of dive-bombers demonstrated dramatically the potential of such

aircraft, not only did the US Navy adopt such tactics as standard for anti-shipping operations, but both Germany and Japan made due note of this information.

Germany's Ernst Udet was so impressed by the potential of dive-bombing that he influenced the development of aircraft with such capability to serve with the Luftwaffe, the creation of which service was announced officially on 9 March 1935. The idea was taken up enthusiastically, to the extent that a special dive-bomber was created, the Junkers Ju 87 Stuka, but the Luftwaffe directed that new bombers being developed by the German industry must also have a dive-bombing capability. There was little support for a long-range strategic bomber, except from the Luftwaffe's first Chief of Staff, Lt.-Gen. Wever. After his death, in 1936, he was superseded by General Kesselring, an advocate of tactical support for the Army, with the result that Germany had no long-range strategic bombers for operations throughout the war. Instead, design and production was concentrated on short-range lightly-armed bombers intended for daylight use. The first standard single-seat fighter to be operated by the Luftwaffe

was the rugged-looking Heinkel He 51 biplane, but this was soon followed by Willy Messerschmitt's superb Bf 109 (later Me 109) single-seat fighter which, in progressively developed versions, was to serve the German air force throughout the Second World War.

Aircraft produced in Italy during this period were mostly of biplane configuration, their performance limited somewhat by the quality of the engines provided to power them. In retrospect, this seems ironic during a period when the Italian aircraft industry was producing some excellent aircraft and powerful engines to compete in the Schneider Trophy Contests. Even after the Macchi-Castoldi 72 had achieved a new world speed record, in 1934, the aircraft industry was instructed to continue the production of radial air-cooled engines for military use. Not until Italy was able to obtain higher-powered Daimler-Benz in-line engines from Germany during the war did production of high-performance fighter aircraft become a reality. Two exceptions to this were the Fiat C.R.32 biplane fighter and Savoia-

Marchetti S.M.79 bomber, both remarkable aircraft. The latter was classed among the best land-based bombers of the Second World War.

Japan had been busy building up the strength of her air forces from the time that the French and British missions had visited that country. The Navy's air arm expanded most dramatically, with new and effective aircraft equipping the six aircraft carriers that were built between the wars.

Germany's announcement of the creation of the Luftwaffe caused great concern in both Britain and France, especially as German propaganda was designed to exaggerate the size and capability of this new force. Immediately, both nations initiated massive re-armament programmes. In the case of Britain it led to the design and development of aircraft such as the Spitfire and Hurricane fighters, and Blenheim and Wellington bombers with which the war was begun, as well as the important four-engine strategic bombers that entered service as it progressed. France was not so successful; her aircraft industry was

newly-nationalised and in a state of disorder, with the result that the only significant new aircraft entered service too late to be of any use in the nation's defence.

Most of the nations which were to become involved in the Second World War had, during the inter-war years, had some opportunity of using their air forces operationally, thus gaining valuable experience. Britain had used her air force for policing and air control in the Middle East and on the North West Frontier. Germany, Italy, Russia and, on a much smaller scale, France and Britain, had been involved in the Spanish Civil War. Italy had been at war with Abyssinia and Albania, Japan with China and Russia. America's policy of neutrality had sufficed to keep the nation from war, but this meant that when war broke out in Europe, on 1 September 1939, the capability of her Army Air Corps was far behind that of the European nations.

WORLD WAR IN THE AIR

THE INVASION of Poland by German forces on 1 September 1939 was not such a shock as the speed and efficiency with which this brave nation, possessing only a small and outdated air force, was ruthlessly eliminated as a fighting unit. The German *Blitzkrieg* technique, with Stuka dive-bombers providing close support for massive Panzer divisions of tanks and armoured vehicles, swept all before it. Within seventeen days it was all over, and Germany and Russia were busy dividing the first spoils of their uneasy alliance.

When the first air raid sirens sounded in Britain, on 3 September 1939, soon after Prime Minister Neville Chamberlain had told the nation by radio that Britain and France were again at war with Germany, most civilians believed that bombs would soon come raining from the sky. This was not surprising, for they had been conditioned to expect it by a concentrated year of Air Raid Precautions, from newsreel pictures of air raids during the Spanish Civil War, and by early BBC reports of the invasion then in progress in Poland.

The Spitfire (*right*) and Hurricane (*below*), were both eight-gun fighters and both powered by Rolls-Royce engines.

Germany overruns Western Europe

But Hitler then had no intention of fighting simultaneously on two fronts, and it was not until 3 April 1940, when there had been time to prepare for the new campaign in the West, that his war machine was unleashed again; first against Denmark, then Norway, Belgium, Holland and France. By June 1940, the German army and air force could stand and look across the English Channel and see their next target—Britain. It was not to prove quite so easy to eliminate.

The year which Britain had gained, when Neville Chamberlain signed the 1938 Munich peace agreement with Adolf Hitler, was put to good use by the RAF and the nation's aviation industry. Worthwhile numbers of eight-gun Hurricane and Spitfire fighters could be deployed against the enemy, and Britain's development of radar, allied to the reporting network of the Observer Corps and RAF Control Centres, meant they could be used with maximum effect. It was not necessary to fly endless patrols in case the enemy attacked. Instead, the fighters could wait and be directed to attack the enemy aircraft as and when necessary.

Contrary to popular belief, Germany

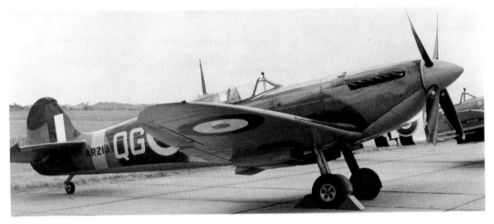

The Spanish-built version of the Messerschmitt Me 109 (*below*) gives an authentic impression of the Luftwaffe's fighter which took part in the Battle of Britain. Opposing bombers are pictured (*opposite*): the Vickers Wellington (*right*) and Dornier Do 217 (*bottom right*) were both used extensively in a variety of roles.

had also developed a radar system, but had not provided the back-up which existed in Britain to direct defending fighters to meet hostile aircraft. In any event, such a comprehensive system proved unnecessary in the first stages of the war, because German defences proved more than adequate to deal with daylight attacks: so effective, indeed, that British bombers could only be sent over German targets by night.

Battle of Britain

Thus, when Germany launched her air force to knock out Britain's air defence, the RAF had some 700 front-line fighters and about 300 more aircraft in reserve, ready and spoiling for the fight which has since become known as the Battle of Britain. By the time it was over, in early September, the Germans had been driven from the daylight sky over Britain: henceforth her bombers had to operate by night. As well as providing a psychological and practical victory for the RAF and the nation it protected, the German Luftwaffe had lost its most experienced pilots.

Space does not permit a detailed coverage of the aircraft involved in the Second World War: instead we must look at the trends which developed as the war itself progressed.

Developments in Britain

Most of the nations which were involved in the war still had biplane aircraft in service at the time of their entry. Britain's air arms all had fairly large quantities of such aircraft, but only the Gloster Gladiator remained in first-line service as a fighter. It was soon to disappear; but one biplane remained in front-line service until after VE-Day, the Fleet Air Arm's famous 'Stringbag': the Fairey Swordfish torpedo-bomber. The Hurricane was gradually superseded by the Hawker Typhoon and Tempest but, in many differing variants, the Supermarine Spitfire remained in service until peace was restored. The Bristol Company, well known for the Blenheim I fighter and Blenheim IV medium-bomber, produced the Beaufighter which enjoyed considerable success as a night fighter and was developed subsequently for use in a wide variety of duties.

The de Havilland Company, long renowned for producing the sensational,

built the 'Wooden Wonder', better known as the Mosquito, which served as fighter, bomber and reconnaissance aircraft, flying high and fast enough so that for most of the war nothing could catch it. Britain had begun in 1936 the development of long-range strategic bombers, resulting in the four-engined Halifax, Stirling and Lancaster bombers which ranged over Germany by night as the war developed. In the initial stages it was the Blenheim, Vickers Wellington and Handley Page Hampden which were the mainstay of Bomber Command.

Regia Aeronautica and the Luftwaffe

Italy, under the dictatorship of Mussolini, had developed its *Regia Aeronautica* into a large air force, and experience gained during its operations in Ethiopia and in the Spanish Civil War should have ensured that it would prove a potent and valuable ally for the Luftwaffe. This did not prove to be the case, for despite the development of some excellent fighter and bomber aircraft, it lacked the *esprit de corps* which distinguished the achievements of the Luftwaffe, RAF, Commonwealth air forces, and the USAAF.

As mentioned previously, the Messerschmitt Me 109 was the Luftwaffe's primary fighter at the beginning of the war. It was to be joined by another superb fighter, designed by Kurt Tank, the Focke-Wulf Fw 190. This aircraft rather dumbfounded the 'experts', who had believed for so long that a fighter must have

an in-line engine if it was to be sleek and fast. Kurt Tank and BMW showed that a properly cowled bluff-fronted radial engine, with air ducted to a cooling fan, could provide sparkling performance, and was free from the weight and vulnerability of a liquid-cooling system. For bombing capability, Germany relied initially upon three medium bombers, the Dornier Do 17, Heinkel He 111 and Junkers Ju 88. The Ju 87 had its initial glory in the first *blitzkrieg* attacks, but was to prove also an important aircraft for deployment against the one-time ally—Russia—which Germany had invaded, with considerable early success, on 22 June 1941. The famous Stuka, however, was slow and vulnerable to enemy fighters, and therefore useless unless Germany was in complete control of the sky.

Russian aircraft production

But like Napoleon before him, Hitler had not appreciated sufficiently the vast areas of land into which the Russians could retreat strategically to blunt the enemy's attack. Neither had he been prepared for the ferocious severity of the Russian winter; and it is doubtful whether anyone could have believed that despite the disruption and chaos of a full-scale invasion, the Russians would be able to move their aircraft industry far behind the fighting areas and resume production surprisingly quickly. From such conditions came a series of Yakovlev fighter aircraft able to confront the Luftwaffe on equal terms.

Supplies of large numbers of fighter aircraft from Britain and the United States enabled the Russian industry to produce other types of aircraft and, in particular, the Ilyushin Il-2 *Sturmovik* ground-attack aircraft. Heavily armoured to protect it from ground fire, the Il-2 was armed with guns, rockets and bombs to provide a most effective tank-destroying capability, taking heavy toll of German armour.

Japan goes to war

Japan, in 1941, had come to the decision that despite the odds the nation's survival, as a result of sanctions imposed by the United States, made it essential for Japan to gain access to supplies of aviation fuel and/or crude petroleum. Indonesia was the nearest source of supply, but this would be available to the Japanese only as conquerors. Cut off from external fuel supplies, Japan's reserves were dwindling rapidly because of the continuing war against China. It was now or never.

At dawn on the morning of 7 December 1941, a Japanese naval task force was steaming close to Hawaii. At 07.40 hours 183 aircraft were over Oahu Island, and streaking to attack Pearl Harbor; as this first group finished its mission, a second wave of 167 aircraft came in to add to the devastation on the ground. Taken com-

pletely by surprise, and while Japanese diplomats were still negotiating peace terms in America, the US Pacific fleet had been virtually eliminated as a fighting unit for some time to come. Happily for the US Navy, its aircraft carriers were at sea, escaping the fate of Battleship Row, where four battleships, two destroyers, a target ship and a minelayer had been sunk; four battleships, two cruisers and a destroyer seriously damaged. When, three days later, the British battleships *Prince of Wales, Repulse* and an escorting destroyer were sunk at sea by Japanese naval aircraft, the beliefs expressed by Billy Mitchell were shown to be valid. No longer could surface vessels afford to ignore the danger in the sky.

Japan had learnt well from the teachings of the Western military missions, especially the Navy which had realised from an early date the potential of the aircraft carrier. And despite the reports which had come to the Western nations from China, none had appreciated that Japan had developed such a wide range of high performance aircraft. They were to discover, in due course, that in many cases this performance resulted from lightweight structures void of armour protection for the crew and without adequate precautions to make fuel and hydraulic systems safe from attack. American pilots soon learned that even if an enemy had superior performance, he needed only to be hit hard once to be turned into a torch. Japanese innovation provided some

American bombers included the Douglas DB-7 (*Havoc* and *Boston*) light bomber (*right*), the most extensively-built and widely-used aircraft in this category. The Boeing B-17 Flying Fortress (*centre*) is known especially well in Britain for its vital contribution to round-the-clock bombing of European targets during WW2. The Boeing B-29 Superfortress (*bottom*), designed to meet the USAAF's requirement for a long-range strategic bomber, proved of vital importance in the closing stages of WW2, destroying Japanese cities with incendiary weapons, and is remembered for its two atom bomb attacks.

The Gloster-Whittle E.28/29 (*left*) was Britain's first aircraft to take to the air under the power of a gas turbine engine, the work of Sir Frank Whittle. The first turbojet-powered aircraft to fly, on 27 August 1939, was the German Heinkel He 178, powered by a gas turbine engine developed by Dr. Pabst von Ohain.

excellent aircraft as the war progressed, but none were more devastating than the *Kamikaze* ('Divine Wind') suicide flights which in the final ten months of the war accounted for no less than 48·1 per cent of all US warships damaged and 21·3 per cent of all ships sunk during the whole of the Pacific War.

America's European/Pacific involvement
American involvement in the war after the Japanese attack on Pearl Harbor meant that, in the long run, success for the Western Allies was inevitable. Even before America was precipitated into battle, the Japanese Navy had expressed the opinion that in a long drawn out war America must win, because of the enormous productive capacity at that nation's disposal.

Britain and the US came to an agreement on production of aircraft: in the main Britain would concentrate on short/medium-range aircraft for combat in the European theatre of operations, while America would build long-range bombers and transport, plus suitable fighter aircraft, with which to fight the long-range island-hopping war in the Pacific Ocean.

Thus, in Europe, British bombers were deployed against enemy targets by night, US bombers by day, to provide round-the-clock attacks. Escorting the bombers over enemy territory by day were such classic American aircraft as the Lockheed P-38 Lightning, North American P-51 Mustang (especially after it was fitted with the Merlin engine) and Republic P-47 Thunderbolt: the escorted aircraft were mainly Boeing B-17 Flying Fortresses and Consolidated B-24 Liberators.

RAF Bomber Command concentrated on large scale attacks by night, with targets pinpointed by Pathfinders which illumi-

nated the bombing area for the masses of Halifax, Lancaster and Stirling bombers following behind. The primary result of such concentrated strategic bombing was to reduce Germany's supplies of fuel to a point where it was impossible to prevent the relentless attacks from the air.

As the war neared its end, both Britain and Germany were to deploy aircraft using a completely new power plant—the gas turbine—which had been developed independently by Frank Whittle in Britain and Pabst von Ohain in Germany. This latter country was also to use operationally the world's first rocket-powered interceptor, the Messerschmitt Me 163B. None of these aircraft were built in sufficient quantity or appeared early enough to have significant influence on operations.

In their final attempts to avoid defeat, Germany launched pilotless V-1 flying bombs and V-2 ballistic rockets against Britain, the base from which British and American aircraft blasted their homeland, and from which the invasion of D-day was launched, but this came too late to have any effect on the final outcome of the war. Overrun, defeated, Adolf Hitler dead, Germany besieged by Britain, America and their Allies in the West, and with the Russians fighting in a devastated Berlin, war in Europe ended on 8 May 1945.

In the Pacific theatre, heroic and bitter fighting by the American Army and Marines had driven the Japanese back towards their home islands. The availability of the Boeing B-29 Superfortress meant that massive incendiary attacks could be launched against Japanese targets. One such raid on Tokyo, on 9 March 1945, destroyed a quarter of the capital, and nearly 84,000 people lost their lives. Five months later, on 6 August and 9 August, the world's first operational atomic bombs were dropped over the cities of Hiroshima and Nagasaki respectively. The prospect of continuing annihilation of Japanese citizens and property on such a scale was inconceivable. On 10 August Japan's leaders decided on immediate surrender, and on 2 September 1945 the documents were signed on board the battleship USS *Missouri*. Six years and one day after Germany's invasion of Poland, the Second World War was over. From first to last it was a conflict which had shown the impact of aviation as a primary military weapon.

KEEPING THE BALANCE OF POWER

AT THE BEGINNING of the Second World War the two main opposing fighters, the Messerschmitt Me 109 and the Supermarine Spitfire, were capable of approximately the same maximum speed at optimum altitude, that is about 571 km/h (355 mph). By the end of the war both had gained 30–40 per cent in weight, had engines with anything up to double the power, and speeds as much as 25 per cent faster, despite the increased weight. In the main, the increased weight came from extra equipment, more armament, and additional fuel capacity to increase range and to cope with the demand of the higher-powered engine.

The problem of compressibility

This was the trend for most aircraft which were in military use over a period of years and, with certain specific exceptions, the increased speed, as well as overall improvement in performance, came from engines of greater power, and more efficient propellers. But as the war progressed and new aircraft entered service, generally improved technology made it possible for level flight speeds in excess of 708 km/h (440 mph) to become fairly commonplace. In the latter stages of the war it was not uncommon for late versions of aircraft such as the British Hawker Typhoon and the American Lockheed P-38 Lightning to exceed these speeds in a dive, their pilots reporting violent shuddering of aerofoil surfaces. In some cases control surfaces, wings and tail units were torn away, and many pilots lost their lives as a result: for the first time they were encountering the effects of compressibility, a phenomenon then known primarily in advanced aerodynamic theory.

When an aerofoil surface approaches the speed of sound, the air ahead of the aerofoil is unable to move aside fast enough, and a shockwave forms both at the leading-edge and trailing-edge of the aerofoil. If it has not been specially designed, not only will the wing (or any other aerofoil surface) be buffeted by this shockwave, but additional drag will also be induced.

Considerable research on this problem was carried out in Germany during the war, especially in relation to the Messerschmitt Me 163 Komet, the world's first rocket-powered combat aircraft which, in the Me 163B-1a version, was capable of a speed of 959 km/h (596 mph) at 3,000 m (9,840 ft). It was discovered that a swept wing, that is one in which the angle between the wing leading-edge and the centreline of the rear fuselage forms an angle of less than 90 degrees, was able to be flown at above-normal speeds without the onset of buffeting. This sort of research information became available to the world's aircraft manufacturers in the early post-war years.

At that time, Britain held a considerable lead in the development of turbine engines, and the RAF's Gloster Meteor F.3s, which were powered by 8·90 kN (2,000 lb st) Rolls-Royce Derwent I turbojets, were the equipment of the RAF's first jet-fighter wing in 1945. The maximum speed of this version was 668 km/h (415 mph); but the piston-engined de Havilland Hornet F.1, which entered RAF service in 1945, had a maximum speed of 780 km/h (485 mph). At that period of time the newly-developed turbine engine had not attained the propulsive efficiency which the engine/propeller combination was capable of at the peak of its development.

Supersonic flight

As the power output of gas turbines began to grow rapidly, it was soon clear that the time was fast approaching when it would be possible for aircraft to travel at more than the speed of sound. This represents a velocity of about 1,193 km/h (741 mph) in dry air at 0°C (32°F), such speed being expressed as Mach 1·0, after the 19th century Austrian Ernst Mach, who studied the propagation of sound waves. Thus, Mach 0·75 represents three-quarters of the speed of sound. Before

new generations of aircraft could travel in excess of Mach 1 as routine, it was necessary to build a research aircraft which would comprise a very strong structure to survive aerodynamic buffeting, and utilise all then-known aerodynamic improvements, together with a powerful engine, to provide the necessary thrust.

Under contract to the National Advisory Committee for Aeronautics (NACA), the Bell Aircraft Company in America designed and built such an aircraft, designated X-1, powered by a rocket engine. Air-launched at 9,145 m (30,000 ft) altitude from a B-29 Superfortress motherplane, this aircraft was flown progressively nearer to the speed of sound by a young USAF pilot, Charles 'Chuck' Yeager. At times the aircraft was buffeted so badly that it seemed an impossible task: then, on 14 October 1947, Yeager slipped through what the media had dubbed 'the sound barrier' to the smoothness of supersonic flight. Subsequently, he flew the Bell X-1A at a speed of 2,655 km/h (1,650 mph), and the knowledge gained from this research was to make possible a whole new range of combat aircraft which was developed all over the world.

The Berlin Airlift

It is unlikely that any serious-thinking person imagined that the Second World War was to prove the 'war to end wars'. It left behind it far too many new and potentially hazardous situations. One of these situations was the partition of Berlin, partly occupied by the Soviet Union, which also controlled the surface routes for transport into and out of West Berlin, which was occupied by British, French and US forces. Clearly, the Russians believed

that by closing the surface routes the Western Allies would leave Berlin and its population to fend for itself. Instead, the city was sustained from the air in an important operation known as the Berlin Airlift, and for almost a year military and civil pilots ferried essential materials and food into Tempelhof, Gatow and, in the latter months, Tegel. The Allies had effectively demonstrated that they were prepared to face any cost to ensure continuing peace. Furthermore, this warning of potential danger to peace in Europe speeded up the formation of the North Atlantic Treaty Organisation (NATO), which took place in April 1949.

The Korean War

The next major trial of strength was to come in Korea when, at 04.00 hours on 25 June 1950, the north Korean infantry, spearheaded by Soviet-built tanks, streamed in their thousands across the 38th Parallel to attack the Republic of Korea. The United Nations Security Council called immediately upon all member nations to assist in repelling the attackers, and troops from many countries were to be involved in bitter combat on Korean soil. In the air the battle was fought primarily by the USAF, USN and RAAF, and in this three-year struggle there came three developments important

for military aviation: a re-birth of aerial reconnaissance, the introduction of tactical air co-ordinators (known later as Forward Air Controllers), and the rapid evolution of the helicopter as a military weapon. There came also, in this conflict, the first air battles between jet fighters.

Large-scale reconnaissance was needed in this new type of war, resulting in the introduction of new techniques and new equipment, as well as the realisation that reconnaissance capability of the highest order would be permanently essential for the prevention of more general war. At the beginning of the evolution of these new techniques was the tactical air

The first operational turbojet-powered aircraft to enter service in the UK was the Gloster Meteor, and the picture (*opposite page*) shows Meteors of the RAAF's No. 77 Squadron operating in Korea. But at that time there was still a lot to be learned about gas turbines and the design of aircraft to reap the full potential of the immense power that such engines promised. In the meantime piston-engined aircraft such as the US Navy's Douglas AD-1 Skyraider (*above*) proved still valuable in post-WW2 conflicts. So, did the North American F-82 Twin Mustang (*left*), developed as a long-range escort fighter. The Fleet Air Arm's Hawker Sea Fury also fought with distinction in Korea, one from 802 Squadron destroying the unit's first MiG-15 on 9 August 1952.

New types of aircraft evolved soon after WW2. Helicopters such as the Bell H-13 Sioux (*left*) proved themselves vitally important in the Korean War. Flight refuelling techniques (*below*) make it possible to deploy aircraft over vast ranges. Spy-planes like the Lockheed U-2 (*bottom left*) can provide important information.

co-ordinator. A pilot and observer, flying in a lightweight aircraft, maintained visual reconnaissance over a battle area until relieved, relaying constantly by radio to an operations centre the state of the battle below. They could call in strike aircraft and direct them to a target, making a very valuable contribution to the battle on the ground. In this conflict rotary-winged aircraft—helicopters— which had seen just a taste of experimental use before the Second World War ended, were to prove invaluable in the kind of war being fought in Korea. Because of their go-anywhere capability, they were able to carry troops and supplies into forward areas inaccessible to any other form of transport. On their return journey to base they could operate as air ambulances, carrying men injured in battle for immediate treatment at field hospitals. By this action, the death rate from wounds in Korea was reduced to the lowest figure then recorded in military history. Helicopters were able to demonstrate also that if armed, even with comparatively simple weapons, they could be developed into an important close-support aircraft for tactical operations.

Cuban Crisis

The Cuban crisis of 1962 was another shock to all nations, threatening a Third World War, and highlighting the importance of reconnaissance in a world which, thanks to the development of a whole armoury of nuclear—or thermonuclear—armed intercontinental ballistic missiles, has achieved the ability to destroy itself. Routine reconnaissance of Cuba had been initiated by the US, after Fidel Castro had shown that close links existed between his regime and the Soviet Union. When surface-to-air missile (SAM) sites of Russian origin were discovered on the island, more intensive reconnaissance showed that Russian-built medium-range ballistic missiles were being installed and trained against the highly-industrial area of the north-east US.

American President John F. Kennedy advised his NATO allies of the situation, launched the massive US deterrent forces into an action alert state and called the Russian bluff. Within a short space of time the missile sites were being dismantled and the weapons shipped back to the Soviet Union.

Importance of reconnaissance

When this crisis was resolved, on 29 October 1962, there was no doubt of the importance of a first class reconnaissance capability, and this desirable aim was pursued energetically by governments all over the world. Not only was the aeroplane involved heavily in such work, but gradually a whole family of pilotless drone aircraft have been developed to carry out such tasks. And as man learned to make his first journeys into space, and evolved the technique of placing satellites into Earth orbit, these too have been given reconnaissance capability, as a part of the delicately-balanced deterrent policy which has so far prevented a nuclear war between major powers, or the beginning of a vast conventionally-weaponed Third World War.

It has not proved adequate—and neither has the gradual development of advanced and potent combat, close-support and strategic aircraft—to prevent conflicts such as that called loosely the Vietnam War, and a host of smaller wars, fought for political, nationalistic and economic reasons, which have plagued mankind since 1964.

Space does not permit a detailed list of military aircraft which have evolved in the post-Second World War years. Instead, it is possible only to mention briefly the trends of development, which have been similar among the major powers. And because, with one or two notable exceptions, lesser powers are unable to face the astronomical research and development costs of a new significant military aircraft,

In the early post-war years came the first of the supersonic fighters. Aircraft such as the US Navy's LTV F-8 Crusader (*opposite, top*) and USAF's Lockheed F-104 Starfighter (*opposite, bottom*) evolved from research programmes that investigated problems of supersonic flight and how to build airframes to fly at such speeds.

New-generation fighters entering service with the world's air forces include the McDonnell Douglas F-15A Eagle air-superiority fighter (*top left*) operational with the USAF; the Grumman F-14A Tomcat (*top right*) is a carrier-based multi-mission fighter of the US Navy, which has swing-wings to cater for carrier landings plus high-speed performance. The Panavia Tornado multi-role combat aircraft (*centre*) will be operational in the late 1970s. The Dassault Mirage F-1 multi-mission fighter (*bottom*) is now in French Air Force use; not only can it fly at Mach 2·2, but it can operate from sod runways.

they too have equipped their air forces with weapons developed by the major powers of the East or West.

Bomber aircraft have grown in capability to the extent that the Boeing B-52 Stratofortresses, still serving with the USAF's Strategic Air Command, have a range of 20,115 km (12,500 miles), to enable them to deliver nuclear weapons against any target in the world. The Soviet Union has nothing in exactly the same class, but has a formidable force of missile-armed strategic bombers capable of posing severe problems to the West if any major confrontation developed.

Most nations, East and West, have short/medium range bombers that would have been regarded as terrifying weapons if available in the Second World War. The French Dassault Mirage IV-A, for example, delivered to the French Air Force in the period 1964–1967, has a maximum speed of Mach 2·2 and can carry 7,257 kg (16,000 lb) of conventional bombs, or a nuclear weapon with a yield of 70KT.

One of the latest close-support aircraft is the US Fairchild Republic A-10A, now entering service with the USAF. Heavily armoured, to protect the pilot from ground weapons, it is armed with a 30 mm seven-barrel cannon which has alternative firing rates of 2,100 and 4,200 rounds per minute, and can carry a maximum external weapon load of 7,257 kg (16,000 lb). Even the 8·69 m (28 ft 6 in) span Anglo-French Jaguar A and S are armed with two 30 mm cannons and can carry up to 4,536 kg (10,000 lb) of external weapons.

It is this weapon-carrying capability, coupled with the speed and agility of these aircraft, which is so impressive. The

Jaguar A or S is a single-seat tactical support aircraft, and yet is able to carry a variety of weapons practically equivalent in weight to the bomb load of early versions of the Boeing B-17 Flying Fortress.

The kind of turbine power which gives this kind of capability can also move a reconnaissance aircraft like the Soviet Union's Mikoyan MiG-25 (code-named 'Foxbat' in the West) at Mach 3·2, or enable an interceptor such as the McDonnell Douglas F-15 Eagle to climb to a height of 29·9 km (18·6 miles) in just

under 3·5 minutes: which is climbing at a rate in excess of 8 km (5 miles) a minute.

To add to the mobility of such aircraft, most have in-flight refuelling capability, so that by planned rendezvous with airborne tankers, they can be given intercontinental range. This has made it possible for air forces to deploy a 'policing' force anywhere in the world at short notice, with long-range transports carrying men and equipment to maintain and operate hard-hitting aircraft that can be in action within hours instead of days.

The British Aerospace (BAe) HS Harrier (*below*) was the world's first VTOL combat aircraft, developed from the earlier P.1127 Kestrel, and in service with the air arms of Spain, UK and USA. The BAe HS Nimrod (*bottom*), developed from the de Havilland Comet, is an important maritime patrol and ASW aircraft.

Both Britain and the Soviet Union have developed jet-propelled fixed-wing vertical take-off and landing (VTOL) aircraft, the Hawker-Siddeley Harrier and Yakovlev Yak-36 respectively, which take-off and land by means of the jet efflux from turbine engines, a transition to forward flight then permitting the fixed wings to provide lift conventionally.

Aircraft of this kind are, obviously, valuable for ship-board operations, but the development of through-deck carriers and improved catapults and arrester gear make it possible for even high performance aircraft to operate from carriers.

The evolution of nuclear submarines, able to deploy ballistic missiles, has brought emphasis to the development of maritime reconnaissance aircraft that have also an anti-submarine warfare (ASW) capability. Thus, Britain's Hawker-Siddeley Nimrod has an endurance of some 12 hours, and is able to detect underwater submarines and launch against them a variety of torpedoes, depth charges, mines and bombs.

Rotary-winged aircraft have been developed to act as flying cranes, work as troop carriers, and act as armed attack aircraft. New generations of jet trainers ensure the training of competent pilots and, in many cases, can be used also as light strike aircraft.

All in all, military aircraft have been developed to a point where they are capable of an almost frightening kill capability. This, on the face of it, would have been abhorrent to the aviation pioneers, who hoped and believed that the aeroplane would be an instrument of peace. Nevertheless, this military potential of the aeroplane has done much to ensure the avoidance of a war between the world's major powers with its potentially catastrophic consequences.

UNIVERSAL TRANSPORT

THE READER will recall that the First World War had done little to improve the airframe structure of aircraft involved. Power plants, however, had been developed from reasonably dependable low-power units to engines of four or five times the power, as well as good reliability.

The Second World War brought about more wide-ranging changes, with extensive improvement in the aircraft's structure and systems. Radar, which had been almost in an embryo state at the war's beginning, developed as a navigational aid, providing an aircrew with a map of the terrain below, which was unaffected by clouds or darkness; radio was not only capable of providing reliable communications on a round-the-world basis, but had been harnessed also to create new and accurate navigational systems and bad-weather landing aids. And America's involvement in the war with Japan, away across the far reaches of the Pacific Ocean, had necessitated the development of transport and cargo aircraft with long-range capability as a priority requirement.

Once again, the persistent cry from airframe designers for more power had resulted in the evolution and production of engines of up to 2,610 kW (3,500 hp). Not only were they more powerful, but most were supremely reliable. In addition, the 'jet' or gas turbine engine had begun its development. Germany had flown the world's first aircraft to be powered by a turbojet—the Heinkel He 178—on 27 August 1939. Britain's Gloster/Whittle E.28/39 had not flown until 15 May 1941, but just over three years later, on 27 July 1944, the twin-engined Gloster Meteor, powered by two 7·6 kN (1,700 lb) thrust Rolls-Royce Welland I turbojet engines, was used in action for the first time. At this early date the gas turbine was already proving a practical engine and would, very quickly, be developed to produce almost unbelievable power.

There was one other contributory factor which had great significance in the enormous post-war expansion of civil aviation: during the war years thousands and thousands of people had travelled by air as routine. They had learned that no longer

The eight-engined Bristol Brabazon airliner, designed to carry 100 passengers, was too advanced to gain sales interest.

was flying fit only for heroes; if transport aircraft were able to carry people from one side of the world to the other for military purposes, then most certainly they would be capable of carrying them around the world on more peaceful business. If air fares were low enough, they would also prove a wonderful means of speeding holiday travel.

End of the flying-boat era

It will be recalled that America had established the first transatlantic passenger services with Boeing flying-boats, and these were maintained throughout the war. Other nations, too, attempted to keep their civil routes open, and even Britain ensured that some long-range links with Commonwealth countries were operated throughout the war. These were really the last years of the flying-boat, for with the return to peace the long-range landplane transport aircraft, which had spanned the

world in military service, were converted hastily for civil use. Suitable airfields, with all essential services, had been built all over the world for the operation of such aircraft, and it made good sense to continue to use these aeroplanes, with which air and ground crews were familiar, for the carriage of fare-paying passengers.

America, which had concentrated on producing long-range bombing and transport aircraft during the war, was in a strong position to supply the needs of civil airlines which would soon be clamouring for passenger and cargo transport aircraft. This factor, plus the pre-war lead they had gained in this field due to the excellence of civil airliners produced by the Boeing and Douglas companies, was to ensure for the United States a lead in this field of aviation which they have retained to this day.

Britain had been aware during the war years that a return to peace would mean a struggle for the British builders and

operators of civil aircraft, and had endeavoured to establish guidelines by means of the Brabazon Committee of 1942/43, which had the task of drawing up plans for the development and construction programmes that would be initiated with a return to peace. The speed of development and innovative progress was such that it was not possible for that Committee to forecast with complete accuracy the post-war needs of civil aviation. As a single example, the Saunders Roe Princess flying-boat, developed as a Brabazon recommendation, was born into a world which no longer needed such aircraft. Perhaps the most important work of this Committee was to encourage designers and manufacturers to take a brief look into the future. If it had done no more than recommend that designer/manufacturers should examine the possibilities of the gas turbine engine, the Brabazon Committee would have been well worthwhile.

In the immediate post-war years, the first generation of airliners were developed from wartime aircraft: the Boeing Stratocruiser (*left*) owed its origin to the B-29. De Havilland in Britain built a new airliner to utilise the newly-emerging and powerful gas turbine engine, the Comet 1. When this failed in service a new Comet 4 (*below*) emerged.

First post-war airliners

So, in the first post-war stage, quick conversions or derivations of wartime bombers served the airlines until the first generation of new aircraft appeared. Thus, in Britain, the Wellington led to the 21/27-seat Vickers Viking, and aircraft such as the Lancastrian, York and Tudor were all members of the Lancaster family. In America, an interim airliner, which evolved from the Boeing B-29 Superfortress, was to prove of great importance when put to work on the North Atlantic route in 1949. This was the Boeing Model 377 Stratocruiser, powered by four 2,610 kW (3,500 hp) Pratt & Whitney radial engines to provide a maximum speed of about 560 km/h (350 mph) and range of up to 6,400 km (4,000 miles). It was followed by aircraft such as the Douglas DC-6 and DC-7, Lockheed L.1049 Super Constellation and L.1649 Starliner. The DC-7C Seven Seas and L.1649A Starliner

represented the piston-engined airliner at the peak of its evolution.

In Britain, new-generation airliners were being developed around the gas turbine engine, in the construction of which power plants this nation then held a considerable lead. First to appear was the Vickers Viscount, the Type 630 prototype of which flew for the first time on 16 July 1948. It had a pressurised cabin to accommodate 32 passengers, and its four 1,029 kW (1,380 hp) Rolls-Royce Dart gas turbine engines each had a reduction-gear drive to a four-blade constant-speed propeller. This type of engine, known as a turboprop, is beautifully smooth in operation, the power unit being devoid of reciprocating components. The expanding gases produced for combustion drive the turbine, and it in turn powers the compressor section of the engine and drives the reduction gear. For speeds up to about 560 km/h (350 mph), such a power plant is more fuel-efficient than a pure jet (turbojet) engine. The Viscount 700 which evolved from the 630 prototype was an immediate success, with accommodation for 47–60 passengers, and a total of 445 were built.

First turbojet airliners

Also in Britain, at about this same time, the de Havilland company were completing the construction of an aircraft to utilise turbojet power plants. This was the Comet 1, the prototype of this flying for the first time on 27 July 1949. The Comet inaugurated the world's first jet airliner service, operated by BOAC on 2 May 1952, on its London–Johannesburg route; soon these aircraft were speeding also between

London–Singapore, London–Tokyo, and in all cases cutting previous scheduled flight-times in half. There was every reason to believe that British manufacturers were in a position to gain a substantial share of the world market for airliners.

Then came disaster, when three Comets disintegrated in flight. Subsequent investigation showed that metal fatigue was responsible for the structural failure, information which enabled aircraft manufacturers across the globe to initiate new fail-safe methods of construction. By the time that de Havilland had incorporated such features into a new Comet 4, Britain had lost its lead in these new-generation airliner types, and has never regained it.

In America, the Boeing company had been busy during this period with the design and construction of a turbojet airliner, and the prototype of this flew successfully for the first time on 15 July 1954. This was the Boeing 367–80, known as the Dash Eighty to all the Boeing family of workers, and known to the world as the superb Boeing 707, of which (together with the similar Model 720) well over 900 have been delivered to airlines all over the world.

From this basic design Boeing have since evolved the short/medium-range 727 with three engines, and short-range 737 with two engines, of which nearly 1,500 and over 500 have been ordered respectively. From McDonnell Douglas has come the DC-8, and Britain attempted, unsuccessfully, to join this big league with the introduction of the Vickers VC10 in April 1964, and larger (163-seat) Super VC10 which went into service a year later.

McDonnell Douglas in America and

The failure of the Comet 1 was due to metal fatigue. From the investigation of this problem manufacturers learned to build new fail-safe structures. Boeing produced the superb Model 707 (*top left*) which serves with airlines all over the world, and evolved a relates series of airliners such as the Model 727 (*centre left*). The Model 747 (*bottom left*) was the world's first wide-body jet, since followed by such aircraft as the Lockheed TriStar, McDonnell Douglas DC-10 (*right*), and the slightly smaller A300B Airbus (*below*) developed by a consortium of European aerospace manufacturers. A long-range version of this last aircraft is now in service.

the British Aircraft Corporation have competed in fulfilling a requirement below that of the foregoing categories, with the introduction of the Douglas DC-9 in 1965 which had accommodation for 80 passengers. BAC's equivalent was the 89-seat One-Eleven, but this latter company has achieved sales of only about one quarter of the nearly 900 DC-9s sold by McDonnell Douglas. Fokker-VFW in the Netherlands has also produced a successful aircraft in a similar category, the 65–85 seat F.28 Fellowship, which entered service first with Braathens SAFE, in Norway, in March 1969.

Russia's national airline, Aeroflot, has followed a similar pattern of development of its civil routes in the post-war years. Ilyushin Il-12 and Il-14 aircraft carried the bulk of air traffic until 1956, when the nation's first jet airliner, the Tupolev Tu-104, entered service on 15 September of that year. It revolutionised air travel in the Soviet Union, offering immense reductions in route times. As in the West, Russian designers have shown interest in the development of turboprop-powered aircraft, attracted by their economical operation, and large numbers of Ilyushin Il-18s have been built. And in the same way that manufacturers like Boeing have evolved a family of long-, medium/short- and short-range aircraft, the Tupolev design bureau have followed a similar pattern with the Tu-114, -124, -134 and -154; similarly, the Antonov bureau have produced a family of civil aircraft for use by Aeroflot.

One trend of more recent years has been brought into being as a result of the enormous cost of designing, developing and producing a completely new aircraft from scratch. This has prompted international collaboration to share the cost, and despite the difficulties caused by varia-tions in language and temperament, it has proved a successful plan, fusing together the best thoughts, ideas and designs of a variety of minds, with different approaches to any specific problem. In the field of civil aircraft, international collaborations have produced such aeroplanes as the technically successful Anglo/French Concorde supersonic transport, and the superb Airbus Industrie wide-body Airbus.

Supersonic transport aircraft

The development of the supersonic civil transport began with agreement between the British and French governments, and between BAC and Sud-Aviation, in November 1962, to collaborate in the development of such an aeroplane. Construction of the first two prototypes began in 1965, the year in which a model of a Soviet supersonic transport, the Tupolev

The ultimate in civil transport at one time appeared to be an airliner that could carry passengers at supersonic speed. The Anglo/French Concorde (*below*) and Soviet Tupolev Tu-144 (*bottom*) are both in service, halving block times by comparison with subsonic turbine powered airliners but proving less economic in operation.

Tu-144, was shown at the Paris Salon. Subsequently, on 1 May 1967, the US Federal Aviation Administration signed a contract with The Boeing Company for the construction of two Boeing 2707 SST prototypes. The American project was cancelled by the US Senate in 1971, by which time the Tu-144 and first Concorde prototype had flown, on 31 December 1968 and 2 March 1969 respectively. On 21 January 1976 Concorde aircraft of Air France and British Airways inaugurated the world's first supersonic passenger services, but the Tupolev Tu-144 had been the first to fly commercially, on 26 December 1975, carrying airmail and freight.

The wide-body transport

Wide-body civil transport aircraft originated in the United States, and an announcement in April 1966 gave the news that Boeing had received a contract for 25 Model 747s for Pan American World Airways. Few then appreciated just what the 747 was all about, but as it became known that its wing spanned 59·64 m (195 ft 8 in), that its 57 m (187 ft) long cabin was 6·13 m (20 ft 1½ in) wide and 2·54 m (8 ft

Large airliners and stylish jet fighters capture our attention, but vast numbers of less exciting general aviation aircraft are important to our everyday life. The DHC Twin Otter (*below*) can provide air services in remote areas; the Taylorcraft Topper (*bottom*) does an equally important job of crop dusting, or spreading fertilizers to boost crop production.

4 in) high, and that it could accommodate up to 500 passengers, the media dubbed it immediately the 'Jumbo Jet'—a name which has stuck.

First entering service on Pan Am's New York–London route on 22 January 1970, well over 300 of these aircraft have since been delivered. They have been followed into service by the McDonnell Douglas DC-10 (5 August 1971), which can seat 380 passengers, the Lockheed TriStar (15 April 1972), which accommodates a maximum of 400 passengers, and the internationally-built Airbus A300 (23 May 1974) which has a seating capacity of 336 passengers.

This latter aircraft, Europe's first wide-body jet transport, has been built and developed by Aérospatiale of France, Deutsche Airbus (MBB and VFW-Fokker) of Germany, Fokker-VFW of the Netherlands, CASA of Spain and Hawker-Siddeley Aviation (now British Aerospace) in the United Kingdom.

General aviation

But aviation is made up of so much more than civil transports, whatever the size of aircraft. General aviation can be regarded

as covering all other aspects of civil flying, and this field has expanded enormously since the war. The 'Big Three' in America, Beechcraft, Cessna and Piper, have collectively built more than a quarter of a million aircraft, the greater percentage of these since 1946, with a predominance of light planes. Beech, for example, has built more than 10,000 examples of its 4/5-seat Model 35 Bonanza; Cessna has produced more than 23,000 two-seat Model 150s; Piper has built more than 40,000 of the

two-seat PA-18 Cub and its predecessors.

In America, the Experimental Aircraft Association has fostered the development of home-built aircraft, helping its members to achieve for themselves the dream of flight. Thousands of these aircraft have been constructed all over the world, some of them of advanced design, some subsequently even becoming production aircraft, but most showing in their standards of construction a loving care that would have gladdened the hearts of the pioneers.

One of the 'impossible' dreams of flight became reality in 1977, when Dr. Paul McCready's Gossamer Condor man-powered aircraft (*left*) recorded a first flight. And it is equally satisfying, in this age of noise, to see an airship such as the Goodyear *Europa* (*bottom left*) making its way serenely through the summer sky.

Rotary-wing aircraft

Designers had attempted from the earliest days of powered flight to build aircraft which could take-off and land vertically. Thus have developed rotary-wing aircraft, important work on the rotating wing being carried out initially by the Spaniard Juan de la Cierva, who designed the first successful autogiro. But it was not until the immediate post-war years that really practical helicopters evolved, developing as rugged and reliable vehicles during the Korean War.

Since that time, such aircraft have, perhaps, come nearest to satisfying the aims of the pioneers, for they have demonstrated a remarkable capability to assist as search and rescue aircraft in both man-made and natural disasters. They carry sick and injured persons from places which are inaccessible for any other form of transport; they dust crops, spread insecticides and fertilisers, rescue the foolhardy, help in construction and logging, simplify the inspection of power lines and pipework, fight forest fires, and help the conservation of our habitat in many ways.

Back into history

More recently, yet harking backwards into aviation history, has come the new sport of hang-gliding, following development of the Rogallo flexible wing and even more efficient Jalbert Parafoil. All over the world young people have been building and flying hang-gliders as an exhilarating sport, perhaps unaware that they are emulating the pioneers who provided the final stimulus for the achievement of powered flight.

An even more exciting event, and one which would have been regarded as a miracle by the pioneers, was the achievement of Dr. Paul McCready in America during 1977. Taking off at Shafter, California, on 23 August, his Gossamer Condor aircraft, powered and controlled by racing cyclist Bryan Allen, was flown in a figure-of-eight around two pylons 0·8 km (0·5 mile) apart. This was the first significant man-powered flight, and won for Paul McCready the £50,000 Kremer Prize which had been so long in finding a home.

One step further back was achieved on 7 January 1973, when Cameron Balloons in Britain flew the world's first hot-air airship. Once again airships have begun to appear in the skies, with examples built in Australia, Britain, Germany, and Japan, as well as the excellent non-rigid helium-filled dirigibles (or 'blimps') built in the

No aviation history, however brief, could end without at least one glimpse into the future. We have not mentioned man's exploration into space. The Space Shuttle orbiter *Enterprise* (*above*) represents a culmination of aerospace technology, being designed to fly in space and the atmosphere.

USA by the Goodyear Tire and Rubber Company, which has produced more airships than any other company in the world—a total of 301.

Hydrogen-filled balloons can still be seen taking part in sporting events, but the summer skies of today are often dotted with the brightly coloured hot-air balloons which take this brief history back to the brothers Montgolfier and Father Bartolomeu de Gusmão.

The somewhat sophisticated controllable kites which have captured the enthusiasm of thousands of youngsters are, perhaps, too representative of modern technology to carry our thoughts back to the beginning of heavier-than-air flight in China many centuries ago. It is the plastic kite, printed with coloured birds and dragons, which links the ages; a modern version of an ancient invention reminding us of the 2,000 years of development which have made possible the brilliant achievements of modern aviation.